Cross-Channel Trade between Gaul and Britain in the Pre-Roman Iron Age

Edited by Sarah Macready
and
F. H. Thompson

Occasional Paper (New Series) IV

THE SOCIETY OF ANTIQUARIES
OF LONDON
Burlington House, Piccadilly, London W1V 0HS
1984
Distributed by Thames and Hudson Ltd

PRINTED IN GREAT BRITAIN AT THE PITMAN PRESS, BATH

Contents

Editorial Note

The fourth in the series of one-day research seminars organized by the Society of Antiquaries was held on 21st May 1982 in the Society's rooms at Burlington House. It was an Anglo-French occasion, devoted to the examination of the trading relationships between Gaul and Britain in the Pre-Roman Iron Age. Professor Pierre-Roland Giot, Hon.F.S.A., of Rennes University acted as chairman and has kindly contributed an introduction and concluding comment to this collection of papers. We are most grateful to Professor Giot for presiding and to all who contributed, in particular to Professor Barry Cunliffe, F.S.A., who originally suggested the theme.

October 1983

S.M.
F.H.T.

Illustrations

Abbreviations

Antiq. J.	*Antiquaries Journal*
Arch. J.	*Archaeological Journal*
Arch. Camb.	*Archaeologia Cambrensis*
B.A.R.	British Archaeological Reports
B.G.	*De Bello Gallico*
B.M.	British Museum
C.B.A.	Council for British Archaeology
C.N.R.S.	Centre National de la Recherche Scientifique
C.R.A.A.	Centre Régional Archéologique d'Alet
E.F.R.	Ecole Française de Rome
J.R.S.	*Journal of Roman Studies*
P.P.S.	*Proceedings of the Prehistoric Society*
R.C.R.F.	*Rei Cretariae Romanae Fautores*
R.G.K.	Römisch-Germanischen Kommission
R.G.Z.	Römisch-Germanischen Zentralmuseum
S.P.F.	Société Préhistorique Française
V.C.H.	Victoria County History

Introduction

Pierre-Roland Giot, Hon.F.S.A.
Chairman

It was an honour and a great pleasure for me to be invited by the Society of Antiquaries to take the chair at their seminar on cross-Channel trade between Gaul and Britain in the Pre-Roman Iron Age, and it is also an honour and pleasure to write a few words of introduction to the collected papers. Provided the papers read are not purely a collection of monologues placed side by side, such seminars are very fruitful occasions of exchange and interpretation of information and of ideas. I am now aged enough to note that in the long run what is often called 'progress' in archaeological thinking is essentially a matter of mode, or of fashion. Ladies have new fashions every season; the usual rhythm for archaeologists is more of the ten-year range. In both cases one comes back from time to time to old ideas, blended in new ways. In reality all the so-called 'new' ideas have already been expressed, possibly shyly, by some antiquarian of the heroic days, and the reshuffling of cards chiefly introduces lots of new and better-established facts.

A very long time ago, in 1954 I believe, I called the tendency of British archaeologists to search on the Continent for the sources of all aspects of the different cultures of Britain, without sufficiently taking into account local and natural particularities and local innovations, the 'insular complex'. This idea was expressed somewhat in advance of its time, before the age of the 'new archaeology' for instance, though already in Britain the then newer generation of archaeologists was just beginning, at first with the Neolithic cultures, to seek alternatives to the invasion hypotheses.

It is certain that the flooding of the Straits of Dover/Pas-de-Calais at some moment during the Mesolithic has complicated matters. But it has created the Mediterranean of the North, an association of seas including the Channel, the North Sea, the Irish Sea and that part of the Atlantic Ocean that the oceanologists like to name the Celtic Sea. Up to a certain point this northern Mediterranean has played a similar role to that of the southern one.

If we leave out of our reckoning not only the migrations of people but also the minor infiltrations of small groups or of individuals, if we no longer trace the spread of ideas, we must stick to matter-of-fact archaeology. In the Neolithic,

1

megalithic chambered tombs were not, of course, transported about Europe, nor were their stones moved further than a few kilometres—with the exception of Stonehenge of course—but we do know of a few stone axes that have crossed the Channel. They all come from Brittany and are well known (four axes of the Breton group A, a dolerite from Plussulien, Côtes-du-Nord, are distributed in Hampshire, Somerset and Worcestershire; two axes of fibrolite, certainly from north Finistère around Plouguin, are known from Cornwall). As I have already many times said or written, all these could have come, together or separately, in a boat or on a raft lost in a storm which drifted over. They form a minuscule sample which contrasts badly with the thousands of such axes found east of the Armorican Massif, in Normandy, Maine, Touraine or Poitou, and further still. They prove rather that during the Neolithic the western Channel was much more a barrier than a link, in spite of the ancient fame of the 'way of the sea'. Of course we should take into account the chances of preservation, of recognition, of the discovery and reporting of such items. Stone axes of recognizable rock are ideal from that point of view. It is a pity there is no equivalent way to test the degree of contact via the Straits of Dover; the jadeite axes of Continental origin may be of some help in resolving this question (or more generally, as I suspect, that of links with the southern North Sea around the Rhine estuary).

With the Bronze Age and the use of solid metal, there was a relatively sudden progress in carpentry and hence in boat-building. It is not surprising that at the same time the material evidence for contacts increases. Although there is no smoke without fire, there is a danger with metal objects of giving too much weight to exceptional items.

If we consider, for instance, the Roman period, we could easily obtain a reliable evaluation of the number of tons of *recorded* imports in Britain of terra sigillata. Even if we multiplied it by, let us say, a hundred, it would still be no more than a few boat-loads. Perishable goods may have been far more extensively traded.

In the Pre-Roman Iron Age there may have been a similar ratio between goods actually exchanged and the number of surviving items. In fact our information is probably even more imbalanced. There is the additional difficulty that there was a time-lag of about 100 years between the Romanization of the two sides of the Channel, and the processes were not comparable. And in spite of better boats, there always will have been a difference between the cross-Channel traffic near the Straits and that along the western sea-routes.

Perhaps the papers of this seminar will illustrate some of these differences.

Relations between Britain and Gaul in the First Century B.C. and Early First Century A.D.

Barry Cunliffe, F.S.A.

The close juxtaposition of northern Gaul and southern Britain has ensured that the two lands have remained in contact, albeit sporadically, throughout much of the prehistoric period. Some indication of these zones of contact in the late second and early first millennium is provided by the distribution of bronze implements and weapons (Briard 1965; O'Connor 1980) and recently more direct evidence of the maritime contacts, in the form of potential wreck sites, has been located off the southern shores of Britain (Muckelroy 1981). The development of the Mediterranean states, particularly those of the Greeks and Phoenicians, towards the middle of the first millennium provided an added stimulus to Atlantic trade in intensifying the consumer demand for tin, a demand which cannot have failed to have made itself felt on the tin-rich areas of the south-western peninsula of Britain.

Documentary evidence for the early explorers and for the developed tin trade has frequently been discussed and need not detain us further.[1] The archaeological evidence is rather more obscure, but the remarkable collection of finds from the Mount Batten peninsula, in Plymouth Sound, is highly relevant. An extensive collection of bronzes and copper ingots shows that the site was of some significance as early as the first half of the first millennium B.C. By the fourth century La Tène I fibulae, disc-footed fibulae of western French or Iberian type, and a collection of knobbed bracelets attest both the wealth of the community and its wide-flung contacts at about the time when the Greek explorer Pytheas was sailing in these waters. Mount Batten is admirably sited to exploit the stream tin and the copper lodes of the southern Dartmoor fringe as well as to serve as a convenient collecting base for commodities trans-shipped coastwise from Cornwall.[2] Disc-footed fibulae have also been recorded from the Cornish cemetery at Harlyn Bay.[3]

While the archaeological and documentary evidence combine to show that the south-west of Britain, Brittany and Atlantic France were bound together in a complex network of trade and exchange extending well into the late first millennium B.C., motivated ultimately by the desire of the Mediterranean countries to acquire metals, there is yet little evidence to indicate cross-Channel contact between central-southern and south-eastern Britain and adjacent parts of Gaul. Indeed, in central-southern Britain, communities seem to have developed socially and economically in isolation from the fourth century B.C. until the beginning of the first. All this changed, however, as Roman influence and control spread throughout Gaul following the establishment of the province of Transalpina in the aftermath of the defeat of the Saluvii in 124 B.C.

Atlantic trade in the early first century B.C.

The foundation of the Province in southern Gaul encouraged an influx of Roman entrepreneurs bent on exploiting the commercial potential of the newly acquired territory. One aspect of this, quickly seized upon by the traders, was the simple geographical fact that the Province sat astride a traditional trade route from the Mediterranean, up the Aude via the Carcassonne gap to the headwaters of the Garonne in the vicinity of Toulouse, thence to the Gironde and the Atlantic. The route was widely used in antiquity as the way by which tin was brought to the Mediterranean ports, conveniently by-passing the Carthaginian-controlled Straits of Gibraltar. Even after the Roman armies had curtailed Carthaginian power in southern Spain at the end of the third century B.C., the overland route would have remained popular because of its directness. The establishment of Roman control over the Mediterranean end of the route as far west as Toulouse meant that Roman merchants could now use the traditional exchange and transport patterns for their own ends. The reconnaissance of the Atlantic routes by Publius Crassus (Strabo, III, 5, 11) and the direct evidence for the export of wine, discussed by Cicero (*Pro Fonteio*, 19–20), show that within the first thirty years of the first century B.C. the entrepreneurs had established a firm hold. The archaeological reality of this trade is vividly demonstrated by the distribution of Dressel 1A amphorae, discussed elsewhere in this volume by David Peacock (pp. 37–42) and Patric Galliou (pp. 24–36).

At the British end of the axis the principal port used by those making the last short-haul crossing from Alet, the Channel Islands and possibly the Cotentin peninsula at Nacqueville, was Hengistbury Head on the Dorset coast (fig. 1). The archaeological evidence for this has recently been discussed in some detail (Cunliffe 1982) and need not detain us further. Suffice it to say that the imported commodities attested on the site were Italian wine, raw glass, and whatever products came in pottery containers made in Armorica, while the potential exports included iron from Hengistbury, non-ferrous metals from the Mendips and the fringes of Dartmoor, and Kimmeridge shale, together with a possible range of archaeological intangibles such as corn, hides and slaves. Evidence of reciprocal exchange in Britain between areas of supply and the port strongly argues for an essentially western British orientation (Cunliffe 1982, figs. 12–14).

Whether or not direct contacts were maintained between Finistère and south-western ports, such as Mount Batten, is a moot point. There is no inherent reason why the longer, direct sea crossing should not have been used. Numerous coins of the Coriosolites from Mount Batten itself, together with Dressel 1A amphorae from

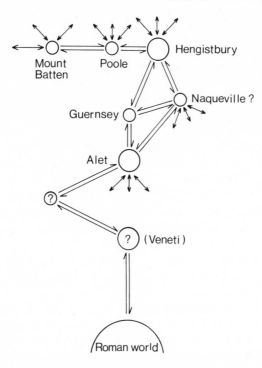

FIG. 1. Diagram showing the relationship of ports along the Atlantic trade route in the period 100–50 B.C.

the Cornish sites of Carn Euny and Trethurgy (*ibid.*, fig. 12), might have come direct from Armorica, but the close links which the archaeological finds suggest existed between Mount Batten and Hengistbury/Poole Harbour (Cunliffe 1983, 125) seem to indicate that short-haul coastal traffic was of importance in linking the south-west with the Hengistbury-Armorican axis. Hengistbury had many advantages, not least the shortness of the sea crossing. It was also admirably sited to exploit the fertile land of Wessex with its surpluses of corn, hides and wool. It may, indeed, have been commodities of this kind that were now attracting merchants in parallel with, or even in preference to, traditional exports such as metals. These questions are difficult to approach on present evidence, but new programmes of excavation may throw further light on the subject.

Reorientation in the late first century B.C.

Several factors combined to cause the dislocation of the Atlantic-Armorica-Hengistbury axis about the middle of the first century B.C. Caesar's campaigns against the Veneti and other Armorican tribes in 56 B.C., which involved the destruction of the Venetic fleet, cannot have failed to have caused serious disruption to traditional trading patterns, but even more far-reaching was the annexation of Gaul by the Romans following Caesar's conquests. With the entire country under Roman control all potential routes could be developed without hindrance and the vast consumer market of Rome was suddenly brought to within a few miles of the British shores. A further factor now coming into play will have been the new political allegiances established between the Roman authorities and the British chieftains. It is even possible that exclusive trading deals were agreed by the Romans, favouring tribes whom they considered to be friendly (Cunliffe 1978, 77–9).

Some indication of the trade routes being developed at this time is provided by Strabo, writing at the end of the first century B.C.

> There are four crossings which men customarily use from the Continent to the island, from the Rhine, from the Seine, from the Loire and from the Garonne, but for those making the passage from places near the Rhône the point of sailing is not from the mouths themselves but from the Morini (IV, 5, 2).

> The crossing to Britain from the rivers of Gaul is 320 stades. People setting sail on the ebb tide in the evening land on the island about the eighth hour on the following day (IV, 3, 4).

> Then [along the Seine] traffic is conveyed to the ocean and to the Lexobii and Caleti; from these it is less than a day's run to Britain (IV, 1, 14).

The details provided are sufficiently explicit to require little comment. Geographically they imply two main points of contact, one in central-southern Britain in the Solent region, the other in the south-east, probably focusing on the Thames estuary, always assuming that sailors preferred to stay within sight of land as long as possible (fig. 2).

Strabo is equally explicit about the goods traded. Exports from Britain included grain, cattle, gold, silver, iron, hides, slaves and hunting dogs (IV, 5, 2), and in exchange the natives were provided with ivory chains and necklaces, amber gems, glass vessels and 'other pretty wares of that sort' (IV, 5, 3). The picture is readily understandable—the Roman consumer market required raw materials and energy in return for which they offered high-value trinkets: it is a familiar pattern.

The archaeological evidence for trade and other forms of contact between Britain and Gaul in the second half of the first century B.C. is sparse and rather difficult to interpret, but certain general trends can begin to be distinguished. Perhaps the most obvious change is in the distribution of amphorae. As Peacock has shown (1971), Dressel 1A amphorae tend to concentrate in central-southern Britain in a zone around Hengistbury, while the Dressel 1B type is predominantly centred in the east of Britain in Essex and Hertfordshire. Although more find-spots can be added to the map, and there is some slight overlapping, the two distribution patterns still remain largely distinct, and since the change-over from Dressel 1A to 1B seems to have been happening towards the middle of the first century B.C. it is reasonable to suggest that the distribution pattern marks a change in socio-economic organization at about this time.

It has been argued (e.g. Cunliffe 1978) that the change marked the demise of the Atlantic route as the result of Caesar's campaigns, but this view is over-simple and in the light of new evidence must now be modified. The new evidence comes from Cleavel Point, Ower (on the south shore of Poole Harbour), and from the recent excavation at Hengistbury. Neither excavation has been published in full, but some of the salient points have been summarized by Williams (1981). Williams has recognized, at both sites, a number of sherds of Dressel 1-Pascual 1 amphorae,

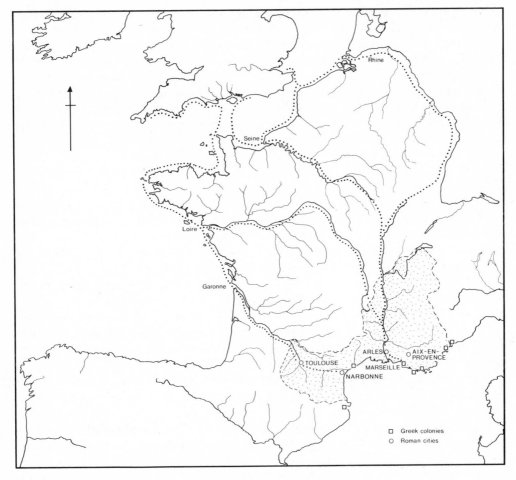

FIG. 2. Trade routes described by Strabo

distinctive products of Catalonia, which were being widely distributed in Augustan times, though they continued in use later. At Cleavel Point the amphorae were found associated with imitations of Tiberian Gallo-Belgic forms and sherds of vessels imported from Aquitania, while at Hengistbury the amphorae were found with local Durotrigian coarse wares stratified above layers containing Dressel 1A sherds and imported Armorican wares. Several sherds of western French origin were found with a similar range of coarse wares. The combination of Iberian amphorae and western French fine wares in post-Caesarian contexts at those two coastal sites is of some considerable significance. That the other finds of Dressel 1-Pascual 1 listed by Williams (1981, fig. 7.2: Knighton, I.O.W.; Owslebury, Hants; Poundbury, Dorset; Bagendon, Glos.; Thaxted, Essex) have a predominantly central-southern distribution, taken together with the several find-spots in Lower Normandy (Deniaux 1980) and the many occurrences in Brittany (Galliou, pers. com.), leaves little doubt that the old Atlantic route was still in operation.

What is, however, particularly interesting is that the bulk of the imported Italian wine was now arriving by a different route focusing on the east of Britain.

It is tempting, therefore, to see the Hengistbury axis as an old-established trade route, thrust briefly into prominence by Roman manipulation in the period 100–50 B.C., falling back to occupy a position of more local significance as soon as more convenient direct routes were developed between the south-east and the Continent following the Roman annexation of Gaul. The conquest and subjugation of the hostile Belgic tribes of north-eastern Gaul in particular will have greatly facilitated the opening up of the Channel to Roman-inspired commerce.

The Seine-Solent axis

This is a convenient, and proper, place to raise an old hare, long dormant—'the Second Belgic Invasion'. The idea that there had been a Belgic invasion of Britain, represented by the bead-rim pottery and associated wares found in Wessex, was first put forward by Bushe-Fox (1925, 33) and was developed in some detail a few years later by Christopher Hawkes and Gerald Dunning in their seminal paper 'The Belgae of Gaul and Britain' (Hawkes and Dunning 1931, 280–309). Briefly stated, they believed that Commius, fleeing from the Romans in about 50 B.C., came to Britain and established control over Hampshire, Wiltshire and Berkshire, setting up a dynasty which was to last until the time of the Claudian conquest. Coming from the Atrebates of northern Gaul, his British domain assumed the same name, reflected in the later, Romanized, name of his capital, *Calleva Atrebatum*. The most evident archaeological sign of the invasion, they believed, was the sudden appearance of bead-rim pottery and related types, analogous to vessels produced in contemporary Normandy.

The hypothesis was not universally accepted. Mrs. Cunnington attacked it within months (Cunnington 1932), and although the authors returned to a spirited defence (Hawkes and Dunning 1932) the 'Second Belgic Invasion' was not so readily accepted into the canons of orthodoxy as were other views put forward in the same paper.

There is little to be gained from discussing the details of this fifty-year-old debate since evidence and attitudes have moved on, but the central archaeological fact remains that there were significant changes in ceramic technology in Wessex towards the middle of the first century B.C., and the flight of the Atrebatic leader Commius sometime about 50 B.C. is surely to be linked with the appearance of coins of Commius in Wessex a few years later. Whether these two disparate observations should be brought into relation with each other is highly debatable: and even if there was a relationship between the archaeological and historical evidence, it is hardly likely to have been direct and monocausal. It is best therefore to consider the two types of data separately.

Mrs. Cunnington in her 1932 attack explained the change in pottery type and technology as the result of new techniques such as wheel-turning being adopted from the Aylesford-Swarling culture of the south-east of Britain. The present writer, considering the same problem in 1966 (1966, 220–1) and subsequently, was of the opinion that the source of inspiration for the ceramic improvement came from the south and resulted from the intensification of trade between Armorica and Hengistbury in the period 100–50 B.C. There is much to be said in favour of this view. Wheel-turning was certainly introduced here at this time, and among the Armorican imports were jars with upright necks and with cordons at the junction of neck and shoulder—a type which, in local fabrics, was to become popular in Wessex in subsequent decades and remained so to the beginning of the Roman era. But a preliminary study of the La Tène III pottery of Armorica has suggested that the problem may be more complicated. Several vessel types, in particular tazze and jars with heavy quoit-shaped pedestal bases, are virtually unknown in Armorica at this time (a point kindly confirmed by Professor Giot) but are well represented in Upper Normandy and the Seine valley. Vessels of this type form a significant component of the first-century B.C.–first-century A.D. assemblages in Wessex[4] and occur in the older collections from Hengistbury. Thus the simplest explanation is that the inhabitants of the Solent shores were in contact with communities of Upper Normandy, and it may well have been that the maritime peoples from this area (the Lexovii and the Caleti) were in regular trading contact with their British neighbours, an axis of contact which, probably in a later guise, was referred to by Strabo (above p. 6).

If this is so Hengistbury is likely to have been on the extreme western edge of this zone, or alternatively may have received pottery indirectly by short-haul coastal trade via a more eastern British port (Selsey?). There is much here that is speculative, but evidence exists that can be tested. The heavy pedestal-based vessels from Hengistbury and other sites in the coastal zone were clearly not made of igneous-derived clays as were the other north-western French imports. Petrological analysis may allow them to be traced to an origin in eastern Normandy. If imported fabrics from this area can be identified at Hengistbury it would be of some interest to see at what point in the sequence they occur—a matter of importance when attempting to discover the chronology of this difficult and involved period.

At the moment all that can be said is that a tentative case can be made out on ceramic grounds for there having been an axis of contact between the Seine and the Solent sometime towards the middle of the first century B.C. The political and cultural nature of the supposed relationship must at present remain purely speculative. The early cremation graves at Owslebury (Collis 1968) present many novel features which could be regarded as intrusive, while the rich burials at Marlborough, Hurstbourne Tarrant and Silkstead, though of the first century A.D., may represent a late expression of an alien tradition adopted by an aristocracy direct from Normandy rather than second-hand via the Catuvellauni of eastern Britain as is usually suggested. The possibilities are intriguing but little more than that.

One way forward in our understanding of these complex issues may lie with a more detailed study of the coinage. The current view (Allen 1961, 116–18) is that Gallo-Belgic F coins, of which only two have been found in Britain, directly inspired British Q and that from British Q developed the dynastic coinages of Commius and those who claim legitimate descent from him—Tincommius, Eppillus and Verica. As our maps will show, the distribution of British Q corresponds well with that of the dynastic coinages (fig. 3a and b), and also with pottery of the kind we have called Atrebatic. A further implication of these maps is that the upper Thames valley must be considered as part of the same cultural-political zone.

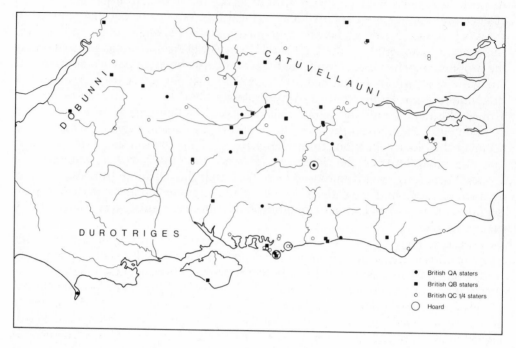

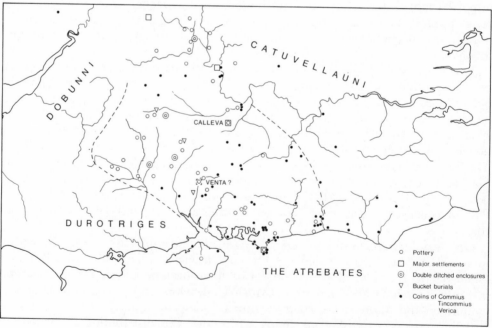

FIG. 3. The Atrebates: above, distribution of British Q coins; below, distribution of later artefacts, coins, etc.

Clearly, there is much more to be done. A new study of the origin and development of British Q, and of the increasing number of Gaulish coins in the Solent area, may well help to clarify matters, while a more precise assessment of the ceramic development within the region will go some way toward providing a more reliable chronology. Changes in settlement form, economy and burial practice urgently need restudy.

Standing back from the ill-focused detail, we can agree with earlier writers that significant social and technological changes took place in a swath of Wessex stretching from the Solent to the upper Thames valley in the first century B.C. and that the area was given a degree of political and economic cohesion, as is shown by the development of coinage within. The least contentious way to view these matters is in terms of the development of an axis of communication between the communities on either side of the Channel leading, perhaps, to the establishment of allegiances such that renegades from Rome, like Commius, could find acceptance. Rather more heretical suggestions will be saved for the final discussion below (pp. 19–20).

Any more detailed study of this problem will have to involve itself with the relevant French evidence—the archaeology of the Lexovii, Caleti and the Veliocasses (fig. 4). Sadly there is little that is new. The cemeteries of Upper Normandy

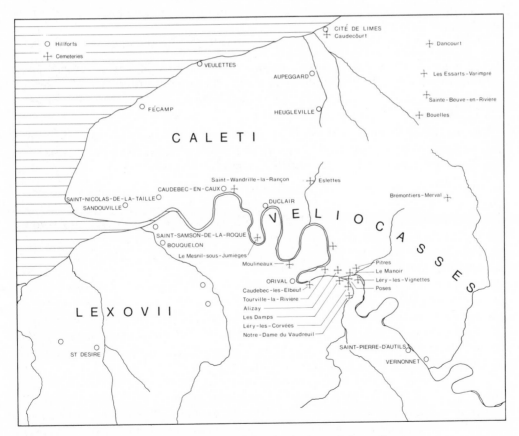

FIG. 4. Archaeological sites in the lower Seine valley

were summarized by Hawkes and Dunning fifty years ago (1931, 196–218) and their assessment, that the majority of the burials belong to the first century B.C. but that some continue until as late as A.D. 70, is incontestable. Wheeler's excavation at the hill-forts of Duclair and Fécamp and his survey of other forts in the region (Wheeler and Richardson 1957) have added further detail, while Dominique Bertin's preliminary study of Iron Age sites in Normandy provides a useful list of all known finds (Bertin 1975). The restudy of some old cemeteries such as Inglemare has offered interesting new insights (Duval 1975a), but the most recent comprehensive survey of the material (Duval 1975b) demonstrates how little has been added to knowledge in the last thirty years. Unless new programmes of field-work and excavation are initiated it seems unlikely that the French data will have much to offer to the problem.

The Somme-Thames axis and the Aylesford-Swarling problem

It is not the purpose of the present paper to indulge in a detailed discussion of the relationship between the south-east of Britain and the adjacent Continent in the 150 years or so before the Claudian conquest, since the literature is extensive and comparatively well known.[5] The essence of the problem lies in the extreme difficulty of collating historical, numismatic and archaeological evidence and of the near impossibility of offering a fine enough calibration of any of the data to make detailed discussion worthwhile.

The relevant historical evidence is restricted to two brief comments by Caesar:

> The coastal areas [of Britain] are inhabited by invaders who crossed from Belgium for the sake of plunder and then, when the fighting was over, settled there and began to work the land; these people have almost all kept the names of the tribes from which they originated (v, 12).

> Within living memory their king [i.e. of the Suessiones] had been one Diviciacus, the most powerful ruler in the whole of Gaul, who had control not only over a large area of this region but also of Britain (II, 4).

Together they imply folk movement and settlement, and the maintenance of political allegiances.

The numismatic evidence is highly complex and is at present undergoing significant reassessment (Kent 1978; Scheers 1977) but the current view seems to be that the vast majority of the Gallo-Belgic coins found in Britain arrived as payments at the time of the Caesarian campaigns, though some may have come in earlier. The situation is neatly summed up by Kent in his concluding remarks to a recent paper (1981, 42): 'my aim here is to suggest that we reject the concept of coinage in Britain linked to invasions or migrations of peoples, and interpret it as the outcome of the interaction of related political and economic events.' At this crucial juncture in the complex and specialized study there is little more an archaeologist can do but to accept the advice!

This leaves the purely archaeological evidence: cremation cemeteries, pottery and a few distinctive metal objects including imported vessels occasionally associated with rich burials. In her exhaustive treatment of the pottery, British and Continental, Dr. Birchall was forced to conclude that no distinctive pre-Caesarian assemblage could with certainty be identified in Britain, though she defined an 'earliest' group from Aylesford for which a pre-Caesarian date was possible (Birchall 1965, 248, 288). Rodwell was more hopeful and attempted to isolate a group of coarse-ware vessels which he called 'earliest Belgic' (Rodwell 1976, 221–37). While his belief that this group pre-dates the appearance of Gallo-Belgic wares in *c.* 15–10 B.C. seems perfectly reasonable, on the evidence he has marshalled there is nothing to require a pre-Caesarian origin. At best we can suggest that the 'earliest Belgic' group is probably largely part of an indigenous tradition which may have its roots as far back as the second century B.C.

Dr. Stead has taken the general discussion several stages further in his discussion of the metalwork from the earliest Aylesford-culture burials (1976). Stead suggests the recognition of two phases: a *Welwyn phase* characterized by the occasional presence of imported metal vessels dated to the second half of the first century B.C.; and a *Lexden phase*, defined by the appearance of Gallo-Belgic wares, starting around 15–10 B.C. A consideration of the brooches and metal vessels associated with the earliest burials, of the Welwyn phase, leads Stead to two highly significant conclusions: first, that no burial can be securely dated earlier than Caesar's expedition; and second, that while pottery and other artefacts of the Welwyn-phase burials have close links with northern Gaul, the more exotic metalwork and the most popular brooch forms are of north Italian origin or inspiration. In other words, such evidence as there is strongly suggests that the Aylesford culture of south-eastern Britain developed in parallel with that of north-eastern Gaul in the post-Caesarian period, the two regions being linked by the exchange of prestige goods of Roman origin.

That no pre-Caesarian phase of the Aylesford culture can yet be recognized does not, of course, preclude the possibility of a Belgic migration into the area (but see pp. 19–20). Indeed the distribution of Gallo-Belgic coinage does suggest a community of interest between the two sides of the Channel in times of stress in the mid-first century, but we must surely now accept that the innovations which define the Aylesford culture—cremation cemeteries, goods associated with wine-drinking, and wheel-turned pottery—most likely result from contacts established in the aftermath of the conquest under the eye of the Roman authorities.

In figs. 5–7 something of the geographical reality of these cultural links is sketched out. The maps are largely self-explanatory. Figure 5 shows clearly the sharp divide, about a north–south axis, which manifested itself in burial ritual in the first century B.C. and early first century A.D. on both sides of the Channel. Figure 6 attempts, in diagrammatic form, to show the concentration of 'Belgic' style pottery dominated by pedestal-based jars, while in fig. 7 certain aspects of the rich burial tradition on both sides of the Channel are plotted. Together the maps indicate a considerable degree of cultural unity which must surely have resulted from the free movement of people as well as goods.

In recent years there has been a considerable body of new research and publication of La Tène II and III sites in northern France, particularly in Nord, Pas-de-Calais, Somme, Aisne and Oise, providing an essential new background for the study where previously little had existed. Space does not permit a discussion of this material but the remarks offered here have been written in full knowledge of what is available in print.[6] When the new discoveries have been assessed and synthesized in relation to earlier finds we should be in a position to contrast the striking differences in cultural traditions in the La Tène II period on both sides of

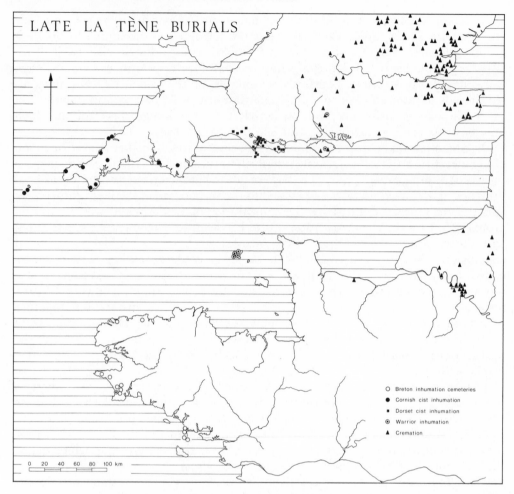

FIG. 5. Late La Tène burial in southern Britain and northern France

the Channel with equally striking similarities after the Caesarian conquest. It may then be possible to approach more carefully the problem of the developments in the two areas in the first half of the first century B.C. What is becoming increasingly evident is the continuation, in Gaul, of native burial rites and pottery traditions long after Caesar's campaigns were over.

The effects of the Rhine frontier zone

The establishment of Roman military bases along the Rhine in the last two decades of the first century B.C., and the Augustan and Tiberian campaigns into the territory of free Germany between the Rhine and the Elbe, put great emphasis on the Rhine, not only as a frontier and a line of lateral communication, but also as a commercial zone consuming raw materials and producing manufactured goods. Thus, under Augustus, the northernmost of Strabo's river routes came into its own.

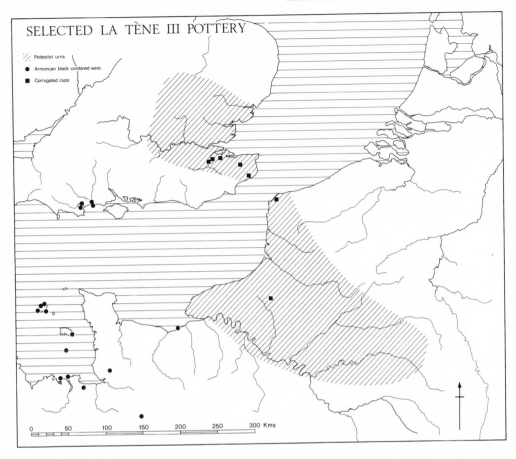

FIG. 6. Distribution of selected La Tène III pottery

In all probability the concentrations of manpower and activity here acted as a magnet drawing off the trade which hitherto had tended to focus on the more southerly river routes.

The recently published excavations of Skeleton Green and of other sites in the neighbourhood of Puckeridge (Partridge 1981) neatly demonstrate the effects of the broader Augustan military policy on trade with Britain. In the period of approximately 15 B.C. to A.D. 25 considerable quantities of imported luxury goods were finding their way to the site: Italian and Spanish wine, north Italian sigillata, mica-dusted jars from eastern Gaul and Gallo-Belgic wares from north-eastern Gaul. Such were the production sources that Partridge was surely correct in suggesting a route from the Mediterranean along the Rhône and the Rhine (via the Saône-Moselle or Doubs rivers) to the Thames (Partridge 1981, fig. 137). It was, no doubt, by way of this route that the considerable quantity of Italian wine was imported in Dressel 1B amphorae to grace the tables of the aristocracy or be buried in the graves of chieftains. The concentration of Mediterranean-inspired prestige goods, associated with wine drinking, in the graves of the nobility of eastern Britain (fig. 8) must, at least in part, have been due to the proximity of their territory to

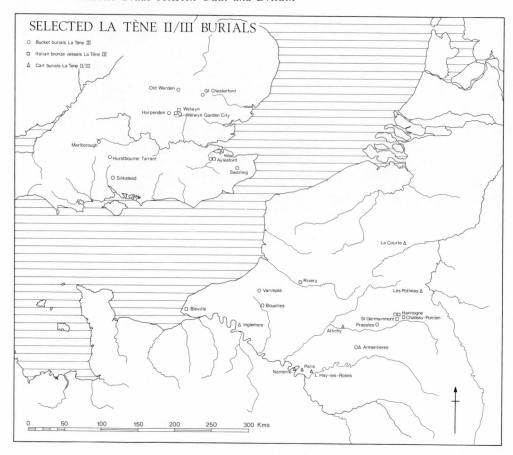

FIG. 7. Distribution of rich La Tène II—III burials

the western extremity of the Rhine route, but a closer examination of the distribution of the rich Welwyn-type burials (Stead 1967; Peacock 1971) suggests that local geographical factors may have been playing a part. The burials divide into three groups: a western group concentrated in the lowland valleys fringing the chalk ridge of the Chilterns; a central group in the region of Welwyn between the rivers Lea and Rib; and an eastern group on the Essex rivers not far from Colchester. On the assumption that the known distribution fairly reflects the actual distribution of rich burials, the pattern presumably reflects the concentration of native power in the last eighty or so years before the Claudian conquest. If native power was based on the ability of its aristocracies to manipulate trade, ultimately with the Roman world, then the burial groups are likely to reflect something of the routes by which commodities passed. Partridge (1981, 351–3) has suggested that one route of importance lay along the Thames and up the river Lea to the Welwyn area. The Verulamium/Welwyn/Braughing aristocracy were indeed very well placed to command commodities passing eastwards across the Chilterns from the clay lands and river valleys to the west where, as we have seen, the western group of rich burials was spread. The pattern is cohesive and could easily be explained in

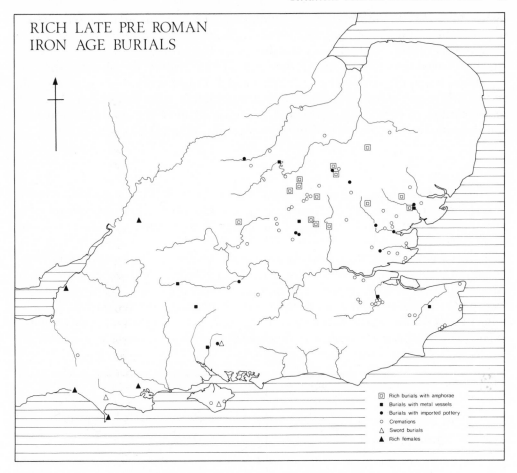

RICH LATE PRE ROMAN
IRON AGE BURIALS

☒ Rich burials with amphorae
■ Burials with metal vessels
● Burials with imported pottery
○ Cremations
△ Sword burials
▲ Rich females

FIG. 8. Rich Late La Tène burials in England

terms of commodities, such as grain, hides and possibly slaves, gathered in the wide peripheral zone, being funnelled to the Lea-Rib confluence for trans-shipment by river and sea to the Rhine frontier. The eastern group, in the Colchester region, could represent the command of a second area of collection and trans-shipment.

The chronology of these developments has still to be worked out in detail but Stead has shown that the Welwyn-group burials belong to an earlier period (his phase I, *c.* 50–10 B.C.) than some of those in the outlying groups which are of phase II (*c.* 10 B.C.–A.D. 50) (Stead 1967, 46–8). While this might indicate a shift in the focus of power, we must await the full publication of the important new excavations in the Braughing-Puckeridge region and at Ware before extending the speculations further.

Standing back from the detail we might distinguish two overlapping systems at work in the period 50 B.C. to A.D. 50; pre-eminent was the exchange of goods and services within an essentially native socio-economic system which bound together the south-east of Britain with northern Gaul in the period following Caesar's conquest and resulted in the development of the Aylesford culture. Superimposed upon this was the more directly commercial Roman-inspired system which required the extraction of raw materials from Britain and in return supplied luxury consumer durables. No doubt this was bound up in a pattern of treaty relationships which involved diplomatic gifts on the one hand and tribute on the other, but the result was much the same—the aggrandizement of those individuals who, through status and geographical location, could accumulate wealth and power. It is the manifestation of these factors, greatly accentuated after the establishment of a stable Rhine frontier, that we dimly recognize in the archaeological record.

Summary

The varied and rapidly changing relationships between Britain and Gaul in the period 120 B.C. to A.D. 50 are summed up in fig. 9. If the arguments presented above are correct all were instigated ultimately by the changing power structure in the Mediterranean world. Before *c.* 120 B.C. the prehistoric patterns of trade and exchange seem to have been centred around the exploitation of metals, one of the dominant routes being the Atlantic sea-ways which linked south-western Britain to Armorica, western France and, via the Gironde-Garonne, the Mediterranean. It was this ancient system that the Roman entrepreneurs manipulated in the decades immediately following the foundation of Transalpina, using wine as the principal export. During this period contacts developed between other territories facing each

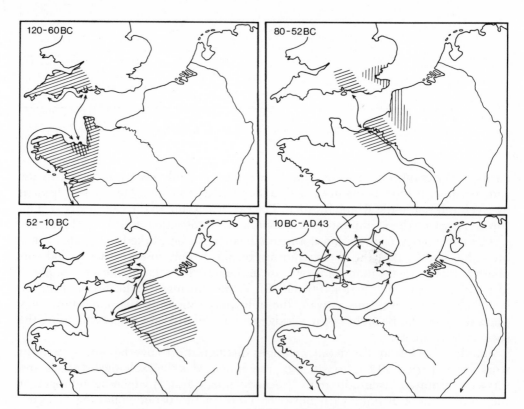

FIG. 9. Summary of the maritime relationships between Britain and Gaul

other on either side of the Channel. A Seine-Solent axis led to significant (pre-Caesarian?) changes in the social and economic structure of Wessex society, while a Somme-Thames axis may have developed in parallel, both resulting in the close allegiance of tribes on either side of the Channel to such an extent that Britons were prepared to help the Belgae in their struggles against Caesar.

After Caesar's subjugation of Gaul contacts between the Belgic area of Gaul and the south-east of Britain were maintained and developed to such an extent that the culture recognizable in the archaeological record on the two sides of the Channel manifested significant similarities. Roman trading practices will have been one causative factor in this, but exchange and other forms of social intercourse were probably still carried out within an essentially native tribal system.

Finally, with the establishment of a stable Rhine frontier during the reign of Augustus (and no doubt the increasing Romanization of the Gaulish *civitates*), British communities came more under the direct influence of Roman traders, which led to the concentration of prestigious goods in the hands of the British nobility who were able to control the movement of commodities required by the Roman administration. The eventual conquest initiated by the emperor Claudius in A.D. 43 brought all this to an end.

The discipline of presenting a view in summary form has the great advantage of highlighting to reader and author alike the severe limitations in the argument (and also in the supporting data). The function of a seminar paper of this kind is simply to offer an approach which can be expanded, modified or rejected as the will of the reader dictates. At best it will have indicated ways in which the ideas expressed may be subjected to further, more rigorous, tests.

Postscript: an even more tentative view

The problem of Caesar's invaders from *Belgium* remains. Put into the perspective of what we now know of the relationships between British and Gaulish communities in the British Late Pre-Roman Iron Age, our inability to identify the invaders is of no great moment. Moreover, assuming that Caesar was correct in his statement, we have no reason to expect such an incursion to be archaeologically recognizable. Even so it still irritates that the only direct reference to migration in British prehistory should prove so elusive.

It is the purpose of this postscript to suggest that we may have been looking in the wrong place. Traditionally, attention has focused on the south-east of Britain where Gallo-Belgic coinage and Aylesford-culture burials and ceramics concentrate. This is understandable and may indeed be correct, but in the current state of research, as we have seen above, coinage is thought to relate largely to gifts and payments made at the time of the Caesarian campaigns, while nothing of the Aylesford culture can be shown to pre-date Caesar. Instead it more readily falls into place as a post-Caesarian development resulting, at least in part, from the more outward-looking attitudes of the Gaulish Belgic *civitates* in the early decades of Roman rule, encouraged, no doubt, by Roman demands for consumer goods. Put another way, the Roman world was using the Gaulish Belgae as trading middlemen until such time that direct contact could be established with the Roman military zone along the Rhine. Although absence of evidence is not evidence of absence, it might be as well to look elsewhere than the Thames-centred area for the Belgic immigrants to have settled.

A few facts may help us refocus:

(a) The Belgae settled in the 'maritime regions of Britain' and retained their tribal names.

(b) Commius, an Atrebatic leader, having led a revolt against the Romans in 51–50, fled to Britain to settle.

(c) Coins of a king called Commius and his successors are found widely in central-southern Britain covering an area which under Roman control ninety years later was divided into two *civitates*, the Atrebates centred on Calleva (Silchester) in the north and the Belgae whose capital was at Venta (Winchester) in the south.

Could it not be that the Roman administrators, in organizing the new province, were telling us precisely where they believed the Belgae to have settled—in the Solent region? There may be some advantage in exploring this glaringly simple solution further.

In political terms, assuming for a moment that an enclave of Belgic immigrants had settled in southern Hampshire early in the first century B.C., it would not be illogical for a war leader of Commius' prestige to be welcomed and allowed to create a kingdom of his own beyond the northern fringe of the Belgic settlement area. The two territories were evidently linked politically in that British Q coins were widely used in both, and only later did the inscribed coinage of Commius' dynasty gain ascendency. The story at least has the advantage of being plausible and can be further tested by a more detailed study of the relevant numismatic evidence.

An immigration of the kind implied by Caesar, with its consequent political, social and economic change, may reasonably be expected to have created recognizable dislocations in the archaeological record. That there were changes in the area under consideration is not in doubt. Cremation was adopted, major innovations can be seen in the ceramic assemblage, hill-forts were abandoned and new defensive structures built, while in the countryside settlement forms underwent radical reorganization. The chronology of the period is, however, still rather ill-focused, but most of these changes can be detected by the middle of the first century B.C. At Danebury the destruction of the hill-fort and the introduction of a new ceramic range associated with Dressel 1A amphorae seems to have taken place about, or not long after, 100 B.C. The archaeological evidence of change deserves more detailed discussion than is here possible (the writer hopes to develop the argument more fully elsewhere).

Changes of the kind outlined do not, of course, prove that a migration took place. In the past the present writer has tended to see them as social and economic manifestations resulting from the development of the Hengistbury-Armorican trade axis, but, as we have hinted above (p. 9), the story is likely to be more complex. However, insofar as they can be legitimately taken together, the archaeological, historical and numismatic evidence does offer a circumstantial case for a migration from the Seine region to the Solent shores in the early first century B.C. Perhaps the only significant mistake which Hawkes and Dunning made in their justly famous 1931 paper was to refer to it as the *Second* Belgic Invasion.

NOTES

1 Most recently by Hawkes 1977, with extensive references. A useful selection of the texts relevant to Britain has been compiled by Rivet and Smith (1979, 49–102).

2 Mount Batten is frequently mentioned in recent archaeological literature but the collection has not been fully published. Summaries of some of the finds have appeared, e.g. Fox 1958 and Clarke 1971. For a note of the potential of the site (with references) and aspirations for the future, see Cunliffe 1983.

3 For the Harlyn Bay fibulae see Whimster 1977. Although fibulae of this kind have their counterparts in Iberia, as is often said, south-western France, on either side of the Gironde-Garonne, is another area in which they are commonly found (Mohen 1980).

4 This is not the place to enter into a detailed site by site discussion of the Late Iron Age ceramics of Wessex, but fig. 3 shows the distribution of sites producing Atrebatic pottery from what may reasonably be regarded as Late Pre-Roman Iron Age contexts. The problem is one to which the author hopes to return on a future occasion.

5 The essential discussions are Hawkes and Dunning 1931, Birchall 1965, Hawkes 1968, Rodwell 1976, Hachmann 1976 and Stead 1976.

6 Some of the literature of more direct relevance to Britain can be listed. For a general review of the Iron Age in the north of France and the Paris Basin, Duval and Buchsenschutz 1976. For more detailed regional surveys: La Tène in Picardie (Duval and Blanchet 1976); Middle La Tène in the Paris Basin (Duval 1976); La Tène material from Oise and Somme (Blanchet and Duval 1975); the cart burial at Attichy (Oise) in context (Duval and Blanchet 1974). For settlement surveys: in the Somme Basin (Agache 1976); *oppida* between the Somme and the Belgian frontier (Leman-Delerive 1980); hill-forts in Picardie (Jorrand 1976). For specific sites: Villeneuve-Saint-Germain, Aisne (Debord 1978); Vauclair, Aisne (Stas 1971); Le Barillet, St. Martin, Oise (Jouve 1973); Verberie, Oise (Agache, Audouze, Blanchet and Lambot 1976); Motte du Vent, Pas-de-Calais (Mariette 1966); Maroeuil, Pas-de-Calais (Leman-Delerive 1971); Francq, Pas-de-Calais (Dilly 1978); Conchil-le-Temple, Pas-de-Calais (Leman-Delerive and Piningre 1981); Allonville, Somme (Fer-dière *et al.* 1973); Port-le-Grand, Somme (Leman-Delerive 1976).

BIBLIOGRAPHY

Agache, R. 1976. 'Les fermes indigènes d'époque pré-romaine et romaine dans le Bassin de la Somme', *Cahiers arch. de Picardie*, iii, 117-38.

Agache, R., Audouze, F., Blanchet, J.-C. and Lambot, B. 1976. 'Verberie (Oise)', *Rev. arch. de l'Oise*, viii, 4–10.

Allen, D. F. 1961. 'The origins of coinage in Britain: a reappraisal', in S. S. Frere (ed.), *Problems of the Iron Age in Southern Britain*, London, 93–308.

Bertin, D. 1975. 'Préliminaire d'une étude de l'âge du Fer en Normandie: inventaire et répartition des sites du Hallstatt et de La Tène', *Ann. de Normandie*, xxv, 227–40.

Birchall, A. 1965. 'The Aylesford-Swarling Culture: the problem of the Belgae reconsidered', *P.P.S.* xxi, 241–367.

Blanchet, J.-C. and Duval, A. 1975. 'Les collections de La Tène provenant de l'Oise et de la Somme au Musée des Antiquités Nationales', *Antiquités Nationales*, vii, 49–58.

Briard, J. 1965. *Les dépôts bretons et l'âge du Bronze atlantique*, Rennes.

Bushe-Fox, J. P. 1925. *Excavation of the Late-Celtic Urn-field at Swarling, Kent*, Soc. Antiq. London Res. Rep. v.

Clarke, P. J. 1971. 'The Neolithic, Bronze and Iron Age, and Romano-British finds from Mount Batten, Plymouth, 1832–1939', *Trans. Devon Arch. Soc.* xxix, 137–61.

Collis, J. R. 1968. 'Excavations at Owslebury, Hants: an interim report', *Antiq. J.* xlviii, 18–31.

Cunliffe, B. 1966. 'Regional Groupings within the Iron Age of Southern Britain', Cambridge Ph.D. thesis, unpublished.

—— 1978. *Hengistbury Head*, London.

—— 1982. 'Britain, the Veneti and beyond', *Oxford J. Arch.* i, 1, 39–68.

—— 1983. 'Ictis, was it here?' *Oxford J. Arch.* ii, 1, 123–6.

Cunnington, B. H. 1932. 'Was there a Second Belgic Invasion (represented by bead-rim pottery)?' *Antiq. J.* xii, 27–34.

Debord, J. 1978. 'Monnaies gauloises de Villeneuve-Saint-Germain (Aisne)', *Cahiers arch. de Picardie*, v, 105–15.

Deniaux, E. 1980. *Recherches sur les amphores antiques de Basse-Normandie*, Cahier des Annales de Normandie 12B, Caen.

Dilly, G. 1978. 'Céramique de tradition de La Tène à Frencq (Pas-de-Calais)', *Cahiers arch. de Picardie*, v, 127–34.

Duval, A. 1975a. 'Quelques aspects nouveaux de la sépulture d'Inglemare', *Rev. Soc. Sav. Hte.-Normandie, lettres et sciences humaines*, lxxvii, 35–46.

—— 1975b. 'Sépultures de La Tène finale et civilisation des oppida en Haute-Normandie', in P.-M. Duval and V. Kruta (eds.), *L'habitat et la nécropole à l'âge du Fer en Europe occidentale et centrale*, Paris, 35–44.

—— 1976. 'Aspects de La Tène moyenne dans le Bassin Parisien', *Bull. S.P.F.* lxxiii, 457–84.

Duval, A. and Blanchet, J.-C. 1974. 'La tombe à char d'Attichy (Oise)', *Bull. S.P.F. études et travaux*, i, 401–8.

—— 1976. 'Le deuxième âge du Fer, ou époque de La Tène en Picardie', *Rev. arch. de l'Oise*, vii, 48–58.

Duval, A. and Buchsenschutz, O. 1976. 'Les civilisations de l'âge du Fer dans le Bassin Parisien et la France du Nord', in J. Guilaine (ed.), *La préhistoire française*, II, Paris, 789–801.

Ferdière, A., Poplin, F., Gaudefroy, R., Massy, J. L., Mermoz, C. and Mohen, J. P. 1973. 'Les sépultures gauloises d'Allonville (Somme)', *Bull. S.P.F.* lxx, 479–92.

Fox, C. 1958. *Pattern and Purpose: a Survey of Early Celtic Art in Britain*, Cardiff.

Hachmann, R. 1976. 'The problem of the Belgae seen from the Continent', *Inst. of Arch. Bulletin*, xiii, 117–37.

Hawkes, C. F. C. 1968. 'New thoughts on the Belgae', *Antiquity*, xlii, 6–19.

—— 1977. *Pytheas: Europe and the Greek Explorers*, Oxford.

Hawkes, C. F. C. and Dunning, G. C. 1931. 'The Belgae of Gaul and Britain', *Arch. J.* lxxxvii, 150–335.

—— 1932. 'The Second Belgic Invasion. A reply to Mrs. B. H. Cunnington', *Antiq. J.* xii, 411–30.

Jorrand, C. 1976. 'Les sites fortifiés préhistoriques et protohistoriques en Picardie', *Rev. arch. de l'Oise*, vii, 59–63.

Jouve, M. 1973. 'La cabane gauloise du Barillet, Béthisy-Saint-Martin (Oise)', *Rev. arch. de l'Oise*, iii, 27–37.

Kent, J. P. C. 1978. 'The origins and development of Celtic gold coinage in Britain', *Actes du Congrés International d'Archéologie: Rouen, 3, 4, 5 juillet 1975*, 313–24.

—— 1981. 'The origins of coinage in Britain', in B. Cunliffe (ed.), *Coinage and Society in Britain and Gaul: Some Current Problems*, C.B.A. Res. Rep. 38, London, 40–2.

Leman-Delerive, G. 1971. 'Une sépulture de La Tène finale découverte à Maroeuil (Pas-de-Calais)', *Rev. du Nord*, liii, 571–7.

—— 1976. 'Le cimetière gaulois de Port-le-Grand (Somme). Essai d'interprétation des fouilles de 1833–1834', *Cahiers arch. de Picardie*, iv, 97–115.

—— 1980. 'Oppida ou forteresses gauloises entre la Somme et la frontière belge: propositions de classement et de chronologie', *Rev. du Nord*, lxii, 791–804.

Leman-Delerive, G. and Piningre, J.-F. 1981. 'Les structures d'habitat du deuxième âge du Fer de Conchil-le-Temple (Pas-de-Calais). Premiers résultats', *L'âge du Fer en France septentrionale*, Mém. de la Soc. Arch. Champenoise, 2, 319–30.

Mariette, H. 1966. 'Le site gaulois de la Motte du Vent à Wissant (Pas-de-Calais)', *Celticum*, xv, 5–71.

Mohen, J.-P. 1980. *L'âge du Fer en Aquitaine*, Mém. S.P.F. 14, Paris.

Muckelroy, K. 1981. 'Middle Bronze Age trade between Britain and Europe: a maritime perspective', *P.P.S.* xlvii, 275–97.

O'Connor, B. 1980. *Cross-Channel Relations in the Later Bronze Age*, B.A.R. IS 91, Oxford.

Partridge, C. 1981. *Skeleton Green. A Late Iron Age and Romano-British Site*, Britannia Monograph 2, London.

Peacock, D. P. S. 1971. 'Roman amphorae in pre-Roman Britain', in D. Hill and M. Jesson (eds.), *The Iron Age and its Hillforts*, Southampton, 161–88.

Rivet, A. L. F. and Smith, C. 1979. *The Place-Names of Roman Britain*, London.

Rodwell, W. 1976. 'Coinage, oppida and the rise of Belgic power in south-eastern Britain', in

B. Cunliffe and R. T. Rowley (eds.), *Oppida: the Beginnings of Urbanisation in Barbarian Europe*, B.A.R. SS 11, Oxford, 181–367.

Scheers, S. 1977. *Traité de numismatique celtique*, II: *La Gaule belgique*, Paris.

Stas, C. 1971. 'Un ensemble funéraire de La Tène III dans le site de l'abbaye de Vauclair (Aisne)', *Rev. du Nord*, liii, 579–618.

Stead, I. M. 1967. 'A La Tène III burial at Welwyn Garden City', *Archaeologia*, ci, 1–62.

—— 1976. 'The earliest burials of the Aylesford culture', in G. de G. Sieveking, I. H. Longworth and K. E. Wilson (eds.), *Problems in Economic and Social Archaeology*, London, 401–16.

Wheeler, R. E. M. and Richardson, K. M. 1957. *Hill-Forts of Northern France*, Soc. Antiq. London Res. Rep. XIX.

Whimster, R. 1977. 'Harlyn Bay reconsidered: the excavations of 1900–1905 in the light of recent work', *Cornish Archaeology*, xvi, 61–88.

Williams, D. F. 1981. 'The Roman amphora trade with Late Iron Age Britain', in H. Howard and E. L. Morris (eds.), *Production and Distribution: a Ceramic Viewpoint*, B.A.R. IS 120, Oxford, 123–32.

Days of Wine and Roses?
Early Armorica and the
Atlantic Wine Trade

Patrick Galliou

Thanks to the pioneering work of such scholars as Fausto Zevi, Miguel Beltrán, David Peacock and André Tchernia, much progress has been made during the last twenty years in the study of Roman amphorae, as increased attention has been paid to typology, kiln material and distribution, as well as to the more traditional approaches to stamps and *tituli picti*. Though the determination of the origin of certain types still poses difficult problems—some amphorae, such as the well-known Dressel 2–4 series, having apparently been produced in a wide variety of places—one may well hope that the added scientific weight of chemical analysis will help overcome these obstacles. Such advances clearly pave the way for a better understanding of the distribution of some staple commodities—wine, fish sauce, olive oil—within the Roman Empire and its neighbouring areas, and will certainly provide archaeologists and historians with invaluable sources of information about ancient economies and trade routes. Recent work in that field, still in progress in France, has concentrated on the setting up of a corpus of amphorae discovered in Brittany, Normandy and the Loire region,[1] as well as on studies of the distribution of individual types.[2] This paper, as a tentative assessment of the wine trade that developed in the Atlantic and the Channel in the Late Iron Age and the first century A.D., has drawn heavily on that work, much of which is still unpublished.

The earliest evidence of a regular long-distance wine trade between the Mediterranean world and Britain and north-western Gaul is shown by the distribution of late Republican or Dressel 1 amphorae which have, in recent years, been discovered and identified in growing numbers on both sides of the Channel (Peacock 1971; Galliou 1982a) (fig. 10). These containers are characterized by a heavy, spindle-shaped body, a long collar and rod-like handles, and a thick fabric, the colour of which varies between a pinkish buff and a dark red, sometimes with a whitish slip. They are between 90 cm. and 110 cm. high and, holding between 20

24

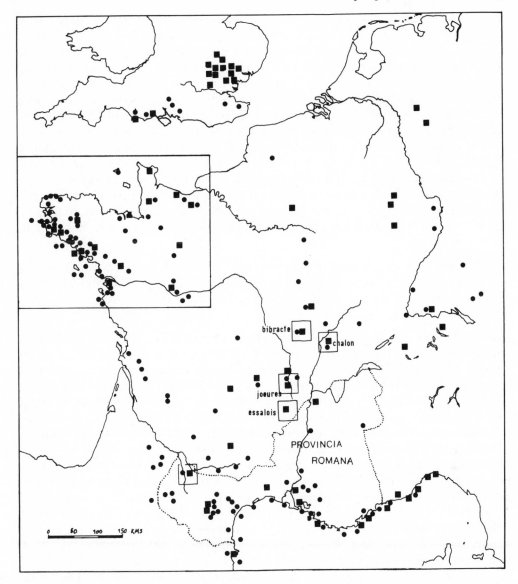

FIG. 10. Distribution of Dressel 1 amphorae in western Europe (after Peacock, revised): ● = Dressel 1A; ■ = Dressel 1B

and 25 litres of wine, may have weighed 50 kg. when full (Labrousse 1968, 144). Nino Lamboglia (1955) has isolated three varieties in the type, two of which show up on the Atlantic seaboard (Dressel 1A and Dressel 1B): Dressel 1A is characterized by a stumpy base, a rounded shoulder and a short rim, triangular in cross-section, whereas the B variety is generally larger, with a long basal spike, a sharper shoulder-angle and a flattish, near-vertical rim. The problem of fabrics, fully analysed by David Peacock (1971), should not detain us here.

Both archaeological discoveries and *tituli picti* securely ascribe the origin of such amphorae to central Italy—Etruria, the Latium and Campania—where Caecuban and Falernian wines were produced in the Roman period (Zevi 1966, 214), and where several kilns, firing Dressel 1A and 1B types together with bricks and *pelves*, have been located (Peacock 1977; Hesnard 1977; Manacorda 1978). Dressel 1 containers thus appear to have been mass-produced in (or near) the large *fundi* owned by the senatorial aristocracy and specializing in the production of wine, which developed from the second century B.C. onwards (Cato, *De Agri Cultura*, I, 6).

The conquest of the Provincia, between 125 and 117 B.C., as a typical colonial venture (Hatt 1966, 37), offered Italy 'un magnifique débouché pour ses vins' (Labrousse 1968, 150–1), and the foundation of Narbo Martius in 118 B.C., some distance from the old *oppidum* of Montlaurès, meant that the age-old route across the 'Gaulish isthmus' could now be opened to Roman traders. The Italian *vinarii* were thus ready to flood the new markets of Gallia Comata, whose inhabitants were known for their passion for wine:

> They are exceedingly fond of wine and sate themselves with the unmixed wine imported by merchants; their desire makes them drink it greedily and when they become drunk they fall into a stupor or into a maniacal disposition (Diodorus Siculus, v, 26, 3).

and were ready to swap one of their slaves for one amphora of Italian best (*ibid.*); all the more so as wine-growing outside Italy had been strictly prohibited by the Senate (Grenier 1934). Cicero's plea for Fonteius,[3] accused as the latter was of *vinarium crimen*, and Caesar's references to the trading (or the non-trading) of wine with Gallia Comata or Gallia Belgica (*B.G.* II, 15; IV, 2; VI, 24) well show that huge sums of money—both private benefits and state taxes—were involved in this trade.

Italian wines were thus directed to the harbours of Cosa (Ansedonia), Ostia or Pozzuoli to be loaded on ships which then sailed to Arelate (Arles) or Narbo, following a southern route between Corsica and Sardinia (Rougé 1966, 94) or hugging the shores of Italy and of the Provincia, as the numerous wrecks discovered and sometimes explored near the French and Italian coasts well testify (Benoît 1954, 1956, 1958, 1960, 1961; Tchernia, Pomey and Hesnard 1978). Narbo Martius being well provided with natural shelters (along the Aude river and in Pomponius Mela's *lacus Rubraesus*), small craft could probably sail up the Aude for some distance (Strabo, IV, 1, 14) before disembarking their cargoes; amphorae would then be loaded onto carts and pack-mules which would proceed along the Narbo–Tolosa trunk road through the 'seuil du Lauraguais' before eventually reaching Tolosa (Strabo, IV, 1, 14; Labrousse 1958; Labrousse 1968, 139–43), the thousands of discarded Dressel 1 containers found in Vieille-Toulouse and Toulouse showing that the town was:

> un grand centre de consommation. Les marchands et les vétérans qui étaient venus de Rome ou de l'Italie pour s'établir dans la ville, n'entendaient ni se priver de leur boisson habituelle, ni des crus qu'ils avaient appris à apprécier (Labrousse 1968, 157).

Amphorae were then again loaded on rafts and flat-bottomed boats that had 800 *stadii* to go before reaching Burdigala (Bordeaux) (Strabo, IV, 1, 14) and the Atlantic Ocean, where they were trans-shipped onto sea-going vessels. The

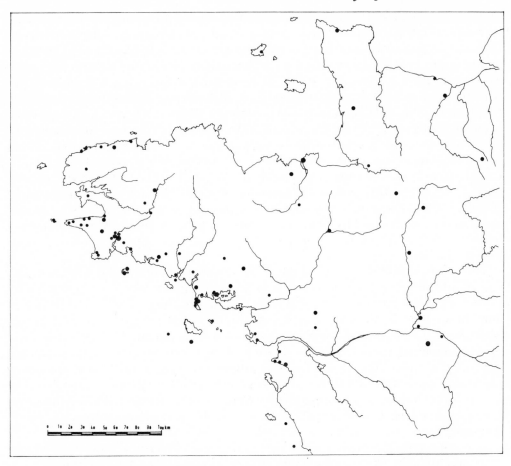

FIG. 11. Distribution of Dressel 1 amphorae in western France: small dots represent single finds, medium-sized dots 2–10 amphorae, large dots over 10 amphorae

prosperity of Burdigala, possibly based in the Late Bronze Age and Early Iron Age on the trading of tin from western Europe to the Mediterranean (Gaudron and Soutou 1961; Etienne 1962), thus progressively came to depend to a large extent upon the trading of wine (Etienne 1962, 98–9). Finds of Dressel 1 amphorae along the western coasts of France (fig. 11) indeed disprove the classic tenet of 'une activité maritime médiocre, purement indigène et locale' (Grenier 1934, 520), and coasters appear to have sold their wine as they sailed northwards towards north-western Gaul and Britain. The discovery of four or five wrecks (or rather of amphorae from probable wrecks) between Bordeaux and Quimper ((1) off Les Sables-d'Olonne (Henry 1973); (2) between Yeu and Saint-Gilles-Croix-de-Vie (Henry 1972); (3) 20 miles off Belle-Ile (André 1959, 66–7); (4) 9 miles south of Belle-Ile (André 1961, 95–7); (5) 2 km. west of the Pointe de Gâvres (André 1959, 65–6)) testifies, however, to the difficulties of the Atlantic route.

Though the overall distribution of Dressel 1 amphorae in western Gaul and the discovery of such containers on small islands of the western approaches of the

Osismi (Iles Glénan–Ile de Sein–Ile Geignog) appear to emphasize the fact that trade ships did indeed sail round western Armorica, matters become much more confused as we reach the north-eastern coast of the Osismi, as no Dressel 1 amphora has ever been found in the western half of the Côtes-du-Nord. This may well mean that the Atlantic trade route veered northwards as it entered the Channel and headed straight for southern Britain, the Saint-Malo area being supplied by the Vilaine–Rance river route, a short-cut across the peninsula enabling traders to avoid the hazards of the circuitous western way. It is, however, very likely that the two itineraries were not mutually exclusive and that, in all cases, the emporium of the Coriosolites at Alet played a central role in the cross-Channel trade, various finds made at Alet and in the Cotentin on the one hand (Langouët 1978) and in the territory of the Durotriges on the other hand (Cunliffe 1978) bearing indisputable evidence of close and regular contacts between the two areas. The Channel Islands, on which a few early amphorae and large numbers of Armorican coins have been brought to light, probably served as midway havens.

The existence and coherence of the Atlantic route having thus been established, one should, however, remember that wine could also reach western Gaul and Britain along another itinerary, and it is clear that the large numbers of Dressel 1 amphorae found in the *oppida* of central France—Essalois, Joeuvres, Gergovie, Mont Beuvray, etc.—or in the Saône at Chalon (Bonnamour 1976, 65) did come up the Rhône (Roman 1974), one branch of this route veering north-eastwards towards the Saône, the Doubs and the Rhine (Vauvassin 1979), and the other north-westwards down the Loire towards Nantes and the Atlantic ocean (Ferdière 1972). Numerous Dressel 1 amphorae have indeed been discovered along the latter route, in Essalois, Châteaumeillant, Levroux or Notre-Dame-d'Allençon (near Angers).

The respective importance of the two trade routes described above is of course extremely difficult (if not impossible) to try to assess. Diocletian's Price Edict, admittedly of a much later date, shows that transport by inland water-ways—of the kind mentioned by Diodorus Siculus in connection with the trading of wine (v, 26, 3)—would be 4.9 times more expensive than sea-transport (Duncan-Jones 1974, 368), which would mean, in so far as costs were concerned, that the Rhône-Loire route could hardly compete with the Atlantic itinerary. One may therefore reasonably assume that political decisions, possibly resulting from Rome's friendship with the Aedui (*B.G.* i, 33) and the latter's feud with the Arverni (*B.G.* i, 31), were instrumental in keeping the former route open. The impact of economic tensions between tribes competing for the juicy taxes levied on such trade should not be underestimated, and they may well have played a part in the events which triggered off the Roman intervention in Gallia Comata. Amphorae indeed appear on the reverse of coins struck by some Gaulish tribes[4] after Roman denarii (Scheers 1969),[5] the best example being the gold staters struck for Vercingetorix (Colbert de Beaulieu 1963, 13).

Most of the Dressel 1 amphorae found in western France have been discovered at a short distance from the sea, and clusters of finds in Quiberon, Quimper and Alet may well point to the existence of ports of trade, amphorae being then distributed to inland settlements by either the river-[6] or the road-system, and to other coastal sites by smaller craft, a system not very dissimilar from the one reconstructed by Barry Cunliffe for Hengistbury Head (Cunliffe 1978, 67–8). Late Iron Age amphora sherds have indeed been found on a large number (about eighty) and a wide variety of sites in western Gaul, in 'towns' (Corseul, Coutances, Jublains, Angers), villages or hamlets, isolated farmsteads, hill-forts of various sizes (*oppida*: Huelgoat, Moulay, Le Petit Celland, etc.; 'fortlets': Mainxe, Plogastel-Saint-Germain, etc.), workshops (briquetages: La Plaine-sur-Mer, Guérande, Baden; ironmaking site: Quimper-Kermoysan) and one temple. This wide spatial and 'social' distribution seems to show that Italian wine was a popular commodity in the Armorican society of the later Iron Age and that most classes could afford it.[7] The presence and the distribution pattern of such amphorae in western Gaul also appear to testify to the existence of an organized market economy in those parts during the later Iron Age, though the well-publicized pre-eminence of the Veneti in the trade between Gaul and Britain (*B.G.* iii, 8; Strabo, iv, 4) is very difficult to ascertain, as most of the Gaulish coins (Allen 1967, 22) and pottery (Cunliffe 1978, 68–71; Cunliffe 1982, 43–5) imported to south-western Britain in the later Iron Age are of north Armorican type. As Allen comments:

> The wide distribution of these [Armorican]coins ... is essentially coastal, obviously the result of seaborne trade. Although Roman historians record the *Veneti* as the carriers of this trade, they have left no substantial coinage to mark their traces (D. Allen 1967, 22).

Most of the coins mentioned above appear to have been minted by the Coriosolites (Cunliffe 1978, fig. 35) and one may well wonder whether, in the first century B.C., trade with Britain was not in the hands of the northern tribe, the Veneti keeping their (vestigial?) hold on the southern façade. This goes of course against the grain of Caesar's and Strabo's evidence, but there is as yet no direct possibility of gainsaying the testimony of the archaeological material.

One cannot of course call the few Republican denarii found in Brittany as witness to the nature of that long-distance interchange, as most of those coins did circulate fairly late into the first century A.D.; besides, most commercial exchanges in these parts must have been of the barter type, though it is still fairly uncertain what Italian wine was traded for. Tin would of course be the obvious answer, and, though Barry Cunliffe has emphasized the meaning of the British evidence (1978, 73–4), there are apparently very few links between the exploitation of Armorican tin and the distribution of Dressel 1 amphorae. Strabo (iv, 5, 2), writing in the first decades of the first century A.D., indicates that Britain produced 'corn, cattle, gold, silver, iron. All these were exported together with hides, slaves and dogs useful for hunting', and as most of those commodities were also to be found in western Gaul, they may equally have been bartered for wine, Armorican salt being yet another possibility. Though Italian merchants were active in Gaul before the conquest (*B.G.* i, 1; i, 39; iv, 2; iv, 20; vii, 3), the pattern of exchange between the Mediterranean world and western Europe must have been fairly limited in scope and based on some kind of irregular trading, its agents being what Rougé has so well defined as:

> des commerçants sans spécialité qui vont de port en port, vendant ce qu'ils ont, achetant ce qu'ils trouvent. Ce sont des commerçants de front pionnier, c'est à dire des commerçants dont la sphère d'action est un pays encore non développé du point de vue économique (1966, 415).

The chronological evolution of that early trade is, however, fairly difficult to assess, as we have very little external dating evidence. Production of Dressel 1 amphorae appears to have begun in the second half of the second century B.C.[8] and to have stopped in the last decade B.C. (Peacock 1971, 165). Nino Lamboglia has suggested relative dates for types A and B based on his own excavations at Ventimiglia, Dressel 1A being predominant in the earliest levels, whereas 1B appeared about 70 B.C., this being confirmed by finds from wrecks (Tchernia, Pomey and Hesnard 1978, 17). It seems, indeed, safe to consider Dressel 1A amphorae as characteristic—in Britain and western France at any rate—of the first half of the first century B.C., whereas 1B would belong to the second half of the century, or more precisely to the years 70–10 B.C. (Peacock 1971, 16); but this has of course only statistical value and no site should ever be dated on the evidence of a single amphora sherd.

Though few of the amphorae found in the West are stamped (Tchernia 1966, 219), most of them, with the possible exception of the Plogastel-Saint-Germain group (Galliou 1982a, 59–60), appear in sites or strata that can be fairly securely dated to the years 80–10 B.C.: Dressel 1A are thus fairly common in pre-Caesarian hill-forts and settlements, whereas 1B amphorae turn up in post-conquest levels and early Romanized contexts, with early terra nigra and Augustan terra sigillata. One obviously cannot reconstruct a systematic trade-evolution pattern on such scanty evidence, but it seems fair to say that, whereas 1A amphorae belong to the pre-conquest phase of contact and exploration, 1B are, to a large extent, characteristic of the early moments of post-conquest Romanization. Interestingly enough, then, 1A amphorae account for 44 per cent of the later Iron Age amphorae found in western France and 1B for only 19 per cent.[9] This is all the more surprising as one would expect the amounts of imported wines to grow during the post-conquest phase of Romanization. The phenomenon may, however, be better understood if one compares it to the distribution pattern of the two types of amphorae in southern Britain (Peacock 1971, fig. 36, pp. 171–9; Cunliffe 1978, 78–9): 1A amphorae are mostly found in the vicinity of Hengistbury Head (Cunliffe 1978, fig. 32), whereas 1B vessels, common in the south-east of the country, are exceedingly rare in the south-west. Both distribution patterns thus appear to corroborate David Peacock's theory of a radical change in trade patterns after Caesar's conquest of Gaul (Peacock 1971, 173). The dramatic uprising of the Veneti in 56 B.C., helped as they were by the neighbouring tribes (*B.G.* III, 8), and the ensuing defeat of their fleet must severely have crippled trade between the two sides of the Channel, Britain, next in line after the conquest of Gaul, being regarded for some time as enemy territory. Thus it is likely that, while western Gaul still received Italian wines, its merchants were forbidden to deal with enemies of Rome, whereas the south-eastern tribes, the Trinovantes and Catuvellauni, had free access to Italian wines as new allies of Rome: the Welwyn-type graves, fairly common in the south-east (Stead 1967), indeed bear witness to that evolution.

The termination of the production of Dressel 1 amphorae in the last decades of the first century B.C. does not, however, testify to a collapse of the long-distance wine trade with Gaul and Britain, but rather to a redevelopment in commercial structures as new products from the Provincia or from Tarraconensis, mass-produced on excellent soils and therefore cheaper than Italian wines, put an end to the former Italian monopoly and triggered off a severe economic competition as they vied for pre-eminence in Gaulish and British markets.

It is fairly difficult, however, to assess with any degree of precision the part taken by each wine-producing region in long-distance exports to Gaul and Britain during the first century A.D., as some particular types of amphora appear to have been produced at the same time in a number of different areas; discrimination between various provenances cannot then be achieved on typological grounds alone, but must obviously be based on a petrological study of the fabrics. This is particularly the case with Dressel 2–4 amphorae, derived in the last decade B.C. from a Greek prototype and characterized by a simple beaded rim and bifid handles, which were manufactured in Italy, north-eastern Spain, southern France and even the Poitiers region to serve the needs of local production.[10]

David Peacock has thus been able to show, by using both surface survey and fabric analysis (Peacock 1977), that Italian Dressel 2–4 amphorae were produced in the same wine-growing regions as Dressel 1 containers—kilns being located at Albinia, in Etruria, and at Sutri (north of Rome)—and that, even though the style of vessels changed radically, exported wines were the same as had been traded in north-western Europe in the first century B.C., this being further confirmed by the study of *tituli picti*. As work on the subject is still in progress,[11] it is hard to tell what proportion of the 200 Dressel 2–4 amphorae so far catalogued in western France (fig. 12) does come from Italy, though most of those amphorae are in a pale buff

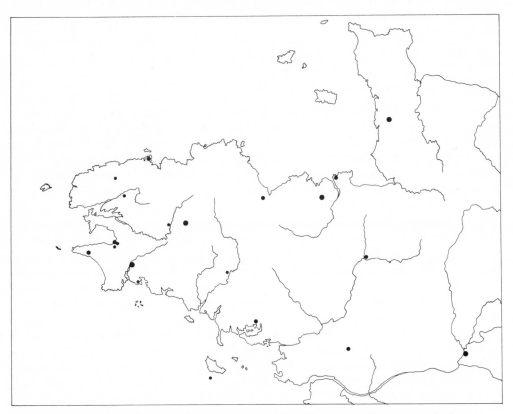

FIG. 12. Distribution of Dressel 2–4 amphorae in western France: small dots represent single finds, medium-sized dots 2–10 amphorae, large dots over 10 amphorae

fabric which apparently excludes any possibility of a northern Spanish origin, and therefore makes it fairly likely that the majority of Dressel 2–4 amphorae exported to western Gaul were indeed manufactured in Italy. We may find further evidence of this in the fact that a small number of other types, whose production may be attributed to Italy, have been found in similar archaeological contexts in the Roman west, this being the case in particular of carrot-shaped amphorae, which have turned up in first-century levels at Exeter, Winchester, Silchester, London, Richborough, Puckeridge, Rennes and Vannes.[12]

A close examination of the fabric of the Dressel 2–4 amphorae found in western France shows, however, beyond any doubt that a small number, characterized by a red-brick fabric with fairly large (up to 2 mm.) white or golden inclusions, were not manufactured in Italy but in north-eastern Spain near Barcelona, in the Roman province of Tarraconensis, famous at the time for its abundant and cheap wines (Martial, xiii, 118; Pliny, *N.H.* xiv, 71) (Tchernia 1971). This obviously testifies to a shift in trade patterns in the late first century B.C. or early first century A.D., which is further corroborated by the spread of another type of amphora, identified in 1960 by the Spanish archaeologist Pascual Guasch, and since then known by the name of Pascual 1 (Pascual Guasch 1960). This type, characterized by an ovoid body, rounded handles with narrow and shallow longitudinal grooves and a high vertical rim (between 6 and 10 cm.), appears in two different fabrics, which have recently been described by David Williams (1981, 128):

> Fabric 1 is hard, rough, dark to reddish-brown with large white inclusions of quartz and feldspar, golden mica and fragments of granite.
> Fabric 2 is softer, smoother, creamy-white with no mica but inclusions of the same nature and size as those of Fabric 1.

The existence of two fabrics does not, in this case, correspond to different areas of production, since both petrology and distribution prove beyond any doubt that Pascual 1 amphorae in the two fabrics described above were manufactured in the same region—and sometimes in the same kilns—as the Spanish Dressel 2–4 (Tchernia 1971, 60), in the territory of the Laeetani, with some outlying kilns in the south-east of the Provincia (Aspiran, Corneilhan), before being exported to other parts of the Empire, with a strong distribution bias, however, towards Aquitania and the Rhône valley.

The distribution of both Dressel 2–4 and Pascual 1 in western France (figs. 12 and 13) shows that the same trade routes were used as had served some decades before for Dressel 1 amphorae, with an obvious scatter of stamped Pascual 1 containers between Port-la-Nautique (Bouscaras 1974) and Bordeaux (Etienne 1962) pointing towards north-western Gaul and Britain. Though few Dressel 2–4 or Pascual 1 amphorae have been discovered in off-shore wrecks,[13] it is certain that such wine-containers were shipped and sold via the same trade routes as Dressel 1 amphorae and fine wares from southern and central Gaul (Galliou 1982b), being unloaded in such harbours as Quimper (100 Dressel 2–4; 45 Pascual 1) or Vannes and then distributed into the hinterland. Both Dressel 2–4 (200 finds from twenty-two sites) and Pascual 1 amphorae (160 finds from thirty-two sites, fig. 14) are fairly common in first-century levels of both urban and rural settlements of western France, where their overall distribution pattern is quite similar to that of the Late Iron Age Dressel 1 containers.

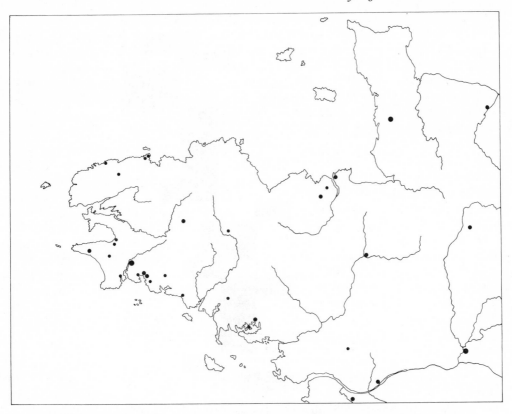

FIG. 13. Distribution of Pascual 1 amphorae in western France: small dots represent single finds, medium-sized dots 2–10 amphorae, large dots over 10 amphorae

This survey of the first-century wine amphorae discovered in western France, which, as work on the subject is still far from being completed, has not included the numerous finds of South Gaulish flat-based vessels of Dressel 28–30 type, points to an obvious shift from the strict Italian monopoly of the first century B.C. to an open and competitive market in the early Principate—Italy, north-eastern Spain and southern France taking their shares of the sales. This should not, however, be interpreted as a sign of decay of the Italian wine-growing complex, but rather as symptomatic of a sharp growth in the demand for wine, resulting from the urbanization of western Gaul in the first half of the first century A.D. and the ensuing spread of prosperity and Roman mores (Tchernia 1971, 81), as it entailed a demand for a wider selection of goods. The distribution of such wine amphorae in Britain (Pascual 1 containers are common at Hengistbury Head and at Cleavel Point, where they occur together with other wares from Central Gaul,[14] and generally speaking in the territory of the Durotriges (Williams 1981), whereas Italian Dressel 2–4 are found in Augustan contexts in south-eastern England, the two distributions being mutually exclusive) is then all the more puzzling as the two types are commonly found in association on French sites, from early first-century contexts at Périgueux[15] or Fléré-la-Rivière (Indre)[16] to Flavian levels in

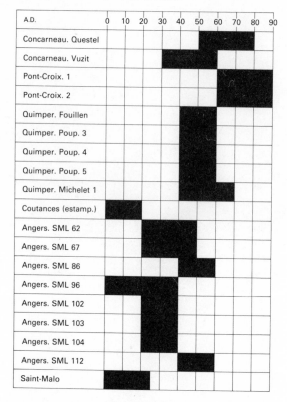

FIG. 14. Chronological distribution of Pascual 1 amphorae found in western France

Quimper.[17] That might mean that

> the south-eastern tribes . . . received . . . Italian wine via the Rhône-Rhine route, while the tribes of the Durotrigian region and surrounding areas possibly obtained Catalan wine by way of the Garonne waterway (Williams 1981, 130)

but we should then be none the wiser as to the presence of Italian Dressel 2–4 in western France, along the Atlantic trade route. This apparent discrepancy might also be explained by a selective embargo on the Atlantic route, while Italian products could reach eastern Britain along the Rhône and the Rhine (finds at Haltern and Oberaden); this explanation is, however, extremely tentative and it is clear that much more work must still be done before we are able to reach any secure conclusion.

Both Dressel 2–4 and Pascual 1 types disappeared in the early years of the second century, but it is obvious that the long-distance wine-trade between the Mediterranean and north-western Europe did not cease, as wine was still shipped in new types of amphorae or in barrels to western Gaul and Britain down to the very end of the Roman period (Galliou, Fulford and Clément 1980), through the Middle Ages and into our times. Roses of the past have withered, but what we drink today, when we enjoy our claret, chianti or vino tinto, is very much old wine in new bottles.

NOTES

1 Under the direction of R. Sanquer.
2 The first volume published is Galliou 1982b.
3 Cf. in particular: *Pro Fonteio*, 9, 20.
4 Cf. E. Murat and A. Chabouillet, *Catalogue des monnaies gauloises de la Bibliothèque Nationale* (Paris, 1889), nos. 9660–3 ('Celtes de l'Est'), no. 1562 (Marseille), nos. 6996–7001 (Turones, TVRO-NOS/TRICCOS type), nos. 3745–9, 3757–9, 3767–9, 3772–80 (Arverni), no. 9879 (Aulerci Cenomani), nos. 6326–30 (Carnutes), nos. 7660–4, 7678 (Meldi).
5 But amphorae rarely appear on Roman Republican denarii; cf. M. Crawford, *Roman Republican Coinage* (Cambridge, 1974), pl. LXVI, 1–2, nos. 378, 385, 396.
6 Cf. the group in central Finistère.
7 But it may equally mean that amphorae, once emptied and discarded, could be reused for other purposes (water containers, etc.).
8 According to the results of the recent excavations at Carthage, Dressel 1 amphorae were imported into North Africa before 146 (information D. Peacock).
9 The remaining 37 per cent cannot be ascribed to a particular sub-type.
10 Cf. in particular: A. Tchernia and F. Zevi, 'Amphores vinaires de Campanie et de Tarraconaise à Ostie', in *Recherches sur les amphores romaines* (Rome, 1972), 35–67; A. Tchernia and J.-P. Villa, 'Note sur le matériel recueilli dans la fouille d'un atelier d'amphores à Vélaux (Bouches-du-Rhône)', in *Méthodes classiques et méthodes formelles dans l'étude des amphores* (Rome, 1977), 231–9.
11 By P. André.
12 Cf. D. P. S. Peacock, 'Roman amphorae: typology, fabric and origins', in *Méthodes classiques . . ., op. cit.*, 264–5. Rennes amphora: cf. R. Sanquer, 'Informations archéologiques', *Gallia*, xxxvii (1979), 373, fig. 22. Vannes amphorae: about eight vessels from an early first-century level (information P. André).
13 Belle-Ile: Dressel 2–4 (André 1959); off Newhaven: Pascual 1 (?), L. Harmand, 'A propos d'un col d'amphore trouvé dans la Manche', *Mélanges Carcopino* (Paris, 1966), 477–89.
14 In particular jars with a mica-gilt slip from Central Gaul (unpublished pottery report from Jane Timby; information P. Woodward).
15 Cf. J.-L. Tobie, 'Périgueux et le grand commerce: les amphores', *Catalogue de l'exposition 'Vésone, cité bimillénaire'* (Périgueux, 1979), 86–7, fig. 56.
16 Cf. *Catalogue de l'exposition 'Celtes et gallo-romains en Berry'* (Châteauroux, 1982), 36–8 (erroneously catalogued as Dressel 1B).
17 Unpublished information from recent excavations.

BIBLIOGRAPHY

Allen, D. F. 1967. 'Celtic coins', in Ordnance Survey, *Map of Southern Britain in the Iron Age*, London, 19–32.
André, J. 1959. 'Trois amphores romaines "pêchées" au large des côtes morbihannaises', *Ann. de Bretagne*, lxvi, fasc. 1, 64–8.
—— 1961. 'Notes d'archéologie sous-marine: amphore romaine au large de Belle-Ile', *Ann. de Bretagne*, lxviii, fasc. 1, 95–7.
Benoît, F. 1954. 'Amphores et céramiques de l'épave de Marseille', *Gallia*, xii, 1, 34–54.
—— 1956. 'Epaves de la côte de Provence: typologie des amphores', *Gallia*, xiv, 1, 23–34.
—— 1958. 'Nouvelles épaves de Provence I', *Gallia*, xvi, 5–39.
—— 1960. 'Nouvelles épaves de Provence II', *Gallia*, xviii, 1, 41–56.
—— 1961. *L'épave du Grand Congloué à Marseille*, Paris.
Bonnamour, M. 1975. 'Le port gaulois et gallo-romain de Chalon', *Mémoires de la Société d'Histoire et d'Archéologie de Chalon*, xlv, 61–71.
Bouscaras, A. 1974. 'Les marques sur amphores de Port-la-Nautique', *Cahiers d'arch. subaquatique*, iv, 103–31.
Colbert de Beaulieu, J.-B. 1963. 'Les monnaies de Vercingétorix', *Gallia*, xxi, 11–75.
Cunliffe, B. 1978. *Hengistbury Head*, London.
—— 1982. 'Britain, the Veneti and beyond', *Oxford J. Arch.* i, 1, 39–68.

Duncan-Jones, R. 1974. *The Economy of the Roman Empire*, London.

Etienne, R. 1962. *Bordeaux antique*, Bordeaux.

Ferdière, A. 1972. 'La vallée du Cher comme voie de relation est-ouest à l'intérieur de la Gaule', *Actes du 97ᵉ Congrès des Sociétés Savantes*, Nantes, 165–79.

Galliou, P. 1982a. *Les amphores tardo-républicaines découvertes dans l'ouest de la France et les importations de vins italiens à la fin de l'âge du Fer*, Brest.

—— 1982b. 'Sigillée de Gaule du Sud en Armorique: diffusion et problèmes', *R.C.R.F. Acta*, xxi–xxii, 117–30.

Galliou, P., Fulford, M. and Clément, M. 1980. 'La diffusion de la céramique "à l'éponge" dans le nord-ouest de l'Empire romain', *Gallia*, xxxviii, 2, 265–78.

Gaudron, G. and Soutou, A. 1961. 'Les racloirs triangulaires de la fin de l'âge du Bronze et la route de l'étain de Nantes à Narbonne', *Bull. S.P.F.* lviii, 583–93.

Grenier, A. 1934. *Manuel d'archéologie gallo-romaine*, ii, 2, Paris.

Hatt, J.-J. 1966. *Histoire de la Gaule romaine*, Paris (2nd edn.).

Henry, B. 1972. 'Le commerce méditerranéen et la Vendée littorale du VIIIᵉ au Iᵉʳ siècle avant J.-C.', *Archéologia*, lii, 67–71.

—— 1973. 'A propos de la découverte sous-marine d'une amphore aux Sables-d'Olonne', *Olona*, lxv, 14–16.

Hesnard, A. 1977. 'Note sur un atelier d'amphores Dressel 1 et Dressel 2–4 près de Terracine', *Mélanges E.F.R.* lxxxix, 1, 157–68.

Labrousse, M. 1958. 'Deux milliaires de la route romaine de Toulouse à Narbonne', *Pallas*, vi, 55–78.

—— 1968. *Toulouse antique*, Paris.

Lamboglia, N. 1955. 'Sulla cronologia delle anfore romane di età repubblicana', *Rivista di Studi Liguri*, xxi, 252–60.

Langouët, L. 1978. 'Les céramiques gauloises d'Alet', *Dossiers du C.R.A.A.* vi, 57–104.

Manacorda, D. 1978. 'The *Ager Cosanus* and the production of the amphorae of Sestius: new evidence and reassessment', *J.R.S.* lxviii, 122–31.

Pascual Guasch, R. 1960. 'Centros de producción y diffusión geográfica de un tipo de ánfora', *Crónica del VII Congreso Nacional de Arqueologia*, Barcelona, 334–45.

Peacock, D. 1971. 'Roman amphorae in pre-Roman Britain', in D. Hill and M. Jesson (eds.), *The Iron Age and its Hill-Forts*, Southampton, 161–88.

—— 1977. 'Recent discoveries of Roman amphora kilns in Italy', *Antiq. J.* lvii, 2, 262–9.

Roman, Y. 1974. 'La place du couloir rhodanien dans la diffusion des amphores de Sestius', *Rev. arch. de l'Est*, xxv, 125–36.

Rougé, J. 1966. *Recherches sur l'organisation du commerce maritime en Méditerranée sous l'Empire romain*, Paris.

Scheers, S. 1969. *Les monnaies de la Gaule inspirées de celles de la République romaine*, Louvain.

Stead, I. 1967. 'A La Tène III burial at Welwyn Garden City', *Archaeologia*, ci, 1–62.

Tchernia, A. 1966. 'Les amphores romaines et l'histoire économique', *J. des Savants*, 216–34.

—— 1971. 'Les amphores vinaires de Tarraconaise et leur exportation au début de l'Empire', *Archivo Español de Arqueologia*, xliv, nos. 123–124, 38–84.

Tchernia, A., Pomey, P. and Hesnard, A. 1978. *L'épave romaine de la Madrague de Giens (Var)*, Paris.

Vauvassin, H. 1979. 'A propos des amphores découvertes à Cersot (Saône-et-Loire)', *Découvertes arch. en Tournugeois*, vii, 61–87.

Williams, D. 1981. 'The Roman amphora trade with Late Iron Age Britain', in H. Howard and E. L. Morris (eds.), *Production and Distribution: a Ceramic Viewpoint*, B.A.R.S. 120, Oxford, 123–32.

Zevi, F. 1966. 'Appunti sulle anfore romane', *Arch. Classica*, xviii, 207–47.

Amphorae in Iron Age Britain: a Reassessment

D. P. S. Peacock, F.S.A.

Over a decade has elapsed since I first considered the question of imports of Roman amphorae into Iron Age Britain (Peacock 1971). During that period the study both of Roman amphorae and also of Iron Age Britain has advanced markedly, so that a reassessment is long over-due. In Britain we have many more finds to consider, covering a broader geographical area and spanning a greater chronological range, while in Northern France developments in Iron Age archaeo-logy have been matched by the work of archaeologists such as Deniaux (1980) or Galliou (1983) who have made a special study of the amphorae. Meanwhile in the Mediterranean there has been a veritable boom in amphora studies and as a result of this we now know much more about the date, contents and origin of all the main types.

It should be clear that the state of knowledge is now very different to what it was in 1971 and that there is a wealth of new evidence to be considered. However, it is neither possible nor desirable to review the entire field in one short contribution and so I propose to concentrate on two facets of the problem. I shall begin by reviewing what we now know about Dressel form 1, since this is undoubtedly the most important type of amphora found in Iron Age Britain and indeed it could be argued that it is one of the most important forms overall. I shall then draw attention to a number of new types which have come to light in recent years. These are particularly interesting because they seem to be filling a notable gap in the early first century A.D.

In 1971 I suggested that the British distribution of Dressel 1 fell neatly into two parts. There was a concentration of finds in southern central England centred on Hengistbury Head, which was the only site in Britain to produce considerable quantities of the early variety, Dressel 1A. The remaining finds were concentrated in eastern England north of the Thames and these were almost exclusively of the later variety, with a collar rim, Dressel 1B. The dating evidence available at the time suggested that Dressel 1A ranged from the late second century B.C. through to the mid-first. Dressel 1B was characteristic of the second half of the first century B.C. In view of this I suggested that the Dressel 1A trade could have been terminated by the disastrous Venetic uprising of 56 B.C., which seemed plausible if one assumed that the trade had been in the hands of the Veneti. However, it seemed equally possible if one assumed direct contact with the Mediterranean, since trade with southern Britain would not have been encouraged after this date, because of support given by British tribes to the Veneti. Since the concentration in East Anglia post-dates Caesar it seemed reasonable to suggest that the luxury trade of the south coast was redirected to East Anglia, where Caesar records an alliance with the Trinovantes. The concentration of amphorae in this area would correspond to the analogous *richesse* in Gaul in the territory of the Aedui, who were also befriended by Caesar.

Unfortunately, this attractive story is difficult to maintain in its entirety today, and there are a number of points about which I am becoming increasingly sceptical. Firstly, however, it is worth stressing that although we now have many more find-sites in southern England, ranging from Kent to Cornwall and northwards to Cirencester and Worcester, the twofold division of the distribution remains broadly true.

The main problem is the date of Dressel 1A, for which we now have much more evidence because of sustained work in the Mediterranean. While this form was certainly current in the first century, it was also very common in the second century B.C. and seems to have evolved from Graeco-Italic types around 130 B.C. (Tchernia 1983). Unfortunately, it is difficult to distinguish the two forms on the basis of rim profiles alone and, in theory, the southern British material could be Graeco-Italic, dating to the second or even the third century B.C. Admittedly, our sherds are more probably Dressel 1A because study of the distribution of complete vessels suggests that the Graeco-Italic form was not exported in any quantity to northern latitudes. Nevertheless, it is as well to keep an open mind. We can either envisage a trickle of imports arriving over a period of at least eighty years, but possibly as long as two centuries, or we can think in terms of more concentrated trade within a limited time span. Either way, correlating the end of trade with the events of 56 B.C. now seems decidedly hazardous. In choosing between a chronologically extended and a concentrated trade-pattern it would be useful to know more of the mechanism of exchange. Are we to envisage Roman ships trading directly with Britain, or were the amphorae obtained from the tribes of northern and western France? My 1971 map badly underestimates the French evidence available even then and it has now been further outdated by the work of Galliou (1983), Sanquer (1971) and Deniaux (1980). The amphorae from Belle-Ile and others from the Atlantic coast must come from wrecks, but since they usually comprise only a single Dressel 1A it is hard to claim in most cases that they are from a Roman wreck, rather than the remains of a native vessel engaged in local exchange. The possibility that Britain received its supplies from northern France now seems more plausible than it did ten years ago. However, there is evidence to the contrary, for very recently I have seen a remarkable collection of amphora fragments from off the Hampshire coast at a locality which cannot yet be disclosed. The finds have been rolled and scattered by the sea, but there is little doubt that they come from a wreck, because the ship's anchor has been found. It is interesting to note that Dressel 1A or Graeco-Italic type rims are certainly present and no native pottery has yet come to light. The case for Roman merchantmen in British waters cannot be dismissed.

The date of Dressel 1B cannot yet be extended in the same way, although I believe there was a period of overlap when 1A and B were produced together. From East Anglia there is a Dressel 1A from Gatesbury Track near Braughing and another from Baldock, but otherwise all the finds north of the Thames are of the B form and should be post-Caesar in large part (Partridge 1979). It is hard to escape the conclusion that these riches were the result of allegiance to Rome, but I may have gone too far in suggesting that the distribution of Welwyn-type graves containing Dressel 1 amphorae maps out the tribal territory of the Trinovantes. Partridge (1981) has recently suggested that the Trinovantes were unable to tell Caesar the whereabouts of Cassivellaunus' stronghold. If Cassivellaunus was chief of the Catuvellauni, the two tribes could scarcely have shared a common frontier, for each would know where the other's centre of power lay. In order to overcome this difficulty Partridge has suggested that there was a block of land centred on present-day Hertfordshire, which separated the two terrains. He suggests that it was occupied by the five named tribes which surrendered to Caesar: the Cenimagni, Segontiaci, Ancalites, Bibroci and Cassi.

This suggestion has certain merits when considering the amphora distribution, for if it really does represent a single territory, one might expect a concentration around the Trinovantian capital at Colchester, falling off towards the boundaries. In practice, however, the map suggests an anomalous concentration around Welwyn, although admittedly the number of points is too small for firm conclusions. Nevertheless the evidence seems to fit, rather better, the concept of two or more political blocks sharing a common allegiance to Rome.

Over the last decade the pace of Iron Age excavation has increased and total retrieval of all material remains has become the norm. This has greatly benefited amphora studies, for the old practice of discarding all but the featured sherds has had a detrimental effect. Amphorae have a very large proportion of body when compared with featured parts, and so to discard body sherds is equivalent to discarding a large proportion of the evidence. Examination of total assemblages has permitted the identification of a number of new types which may have been missed in earlier work. Of these, the most important is the Spanish form, Dressel 1-Pascual 1, first described from Britain by Williams (1981). Dressel 1-Pascual 1 was produced in Catalonia, where a number of kiln sites are known from the Barcelona region. The form is rather similar to Dressel 1B, which it is clearly imitating, but it can be distinguished by its characteristic fabrics and by the vertical grooving down the handles. On the Continent the form dates from the Augustan period until at least the destruction of Pompeii in A.D. 79, but in Britain all finds are from Iron Age sites and none has yet been found securely stratified in post-conquest deposits. Some may be revealed by future work, but it begins to appear that the main thrust of importation was in Augustan and Tiberian times. Williams lists some seven sites, to which can be added an unstratified spike in Colchester Museum, although this could belong to the form Dressel 2–4. It is interesting to note that the form has been recorded from northern France (Deniaux 1980; Galliou 1983) and so the British material would have arrived by cross-Channel trade.

Another form which appears in Tiberian contexts in Britain is Dressel 6. It has been found at Skeleton Green, Hertfordshire, in deposits dated *c.* A.D. 25–45. I am now less cautious about this identification than I appear in the report (Partridge

1981). It has generally been held that this contained the renowned olive oil of Istria, but wine and other commodities may have been carried at times. Buchi (1971) has identified two varieties, labelled A and B, but I am not yet able to make this distinction in small fragments. At present Dressel 6 is very rare and possibly limited to one site.

The most important oil amphora on British Iron Age sites is Dressel 20 from the Guadalquivir region of southern Spain, best known from its abundant occurrences on British post-conquest sites. Hawkes and Hull (1947) first drew attention to pre-Roman imports of Dressel 20, when they recorded two instances in period I at Camulodunum dated *c.* A.D. 10–43. However, Parker (1971) has since suggested that this may be a substantial underestimate. This view is supported by more recent work, because Dressel 20 is proving to be an important component of Iron Age assemblages in Hertfordshire. At Skeleton Green Dressel 20 comprises about 30 per cent by weight of all the amphorae imported in the first century A.D. before the Roman conquest. Similar quantities are present at Gatesbury Track and in other less well-dated sites such as Foxholes Farm, Puckeridge, and in the Henderson Collection from Braughing (Partridge 1979, 1981). In addition Dressel 20 occurs in potential Iron Age levels at Owslebury, Hengistbury and at Cleavel Point, all in southern England (information J. Collis and P. Woodward).

The use of olive oil by the Late Iron Age communities of Britain is at first sight somewhat surprising, for oil was one of the essentials of the Roman way of life which one might expect to be introduced as a result of cultural changes after the conquest. And yet the use of olive oil could date back to the Augustan period, because we have two examples of the prototype of Dressel 20, a more ovoid form generally known as Oberaden 83. One of the British examples was excavated many years ago by the Wheelers (1936, fig. 13) at Prae Wood, while another has recently been recovered from Gatesbury Track (Partridge 1979, fig. 34, 4). It is not entirely clear when Oberaden 83 developed into the typical globular Dressel 20, but it is the latter form that is characteristic of our later Iron Age assemblages, although admittedly the two types can be difficult to tell apart in very small fragments.

Recently Williams and I have attempted to study the pattern of Dressel 20 importation over the Iron Age and throughout the Roman period by examining quantified amphora assemblages which can be dated on other evidence (Williams and Peacock, forthcoming). Our sample has been drawn from thirty-three sites of widely differing types, spread throughout the country. Since this is basically a Roman rather than an Iron Age question, it would be inappropriate to discuss the problems of data retrieval and interpretation, but the graph (fig. 15) summarizes this work and comprises a 'best estimate' based on the evidence currently available.

It must be stressed that the graph does not illustrate the rise and decline of Dressel 20 in *absolute* quantities, but if it were possible to construct such a curve it would probably describe a similar course. Instead it illustrates the changing proportion of Dressel 20. In other words, it does not illustrate changes in the number of ships arriving in Britain, but simply that there were changes in the proportion of cargo given over to Baetican oil.

The graph attests the importance of olive oil in pre-Roman Britain and its somewhat increased popularity after the conquest. During the second century there is a linear rise in popularity followed by a decline in the third century. The

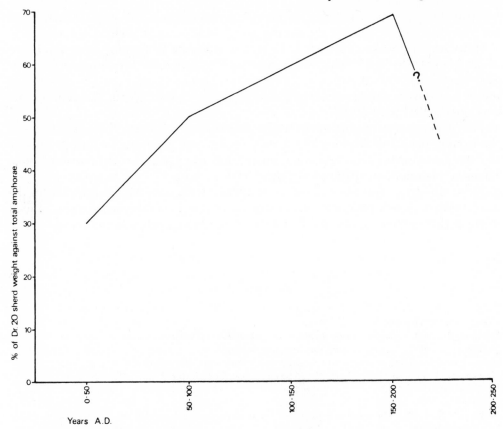

FIG. 15. Graph showing an estimate of the relative quantities of Dressel 20 imports into Britain at different periods

interesting point about this graph is that it is almost exactly paralleled in the Mediterranean. This is illustrated by the quantified sequence of Dressel 20 from Ostia (Panella 1973; Riley 1982). However, even more striking is Pascual's (1980, fig. 4) graph illustrating the proportion of Dressel 20 present on Mediterranean wrecks, for this is an almost exact replica of the British curve. The interesting conclusion to be drawn from this analogy is that the conquest and development of Roman Britain had virtually no impact on the composition of cargoes arriving in the country: the changes noted in Britain are part of a more general phenomenon. Looked at another way, it appears that Iron Age Britain was receiving its due proportion of Baetican oil, and was treated as though it was already part of the empire. No attempt was made to design specific cargoes for the British market, which presumably indicates that the requirements of at least eastern England were not all that different from those of the Roman world.

One further point can be drawn from Pascual's data, since he also indicates the trend in amphorae bearing fish products over the same period. In Mediterranean wrecks, these are in excess of olive oil until the later second century, despite a marked dip in popularity in the later first century. There are very few data to confirm this from elsewhere, but in Flavian levels at Ostia fish-product amphorae are present in about the same quantity as oil containers (Panella 1973, 620).

However, this does not appear to be true of Iron Age Britain, because amphorae of the form Dressel 7–11, which contained such commodities, are much scarcer. At Skeleton Green, for example, they comprise a mere 12 per cent, by weight, of amphorae dated A.D. 25–45, compared with the figure of 30 per cent for oil containers (Partridge 1981).

This is not, however, just an Iron Age phenomenon, because the same is true of the Roman period in Britain, and it may be the case generally in Europe outside the Mediterranean area. At Vindonissa, for example, the proportions seem remarkably similar to Britain (Ettlinger 1977).

Although Iron Age Britain does contrast with the Mediterranean in its consumption of fish products, it is again part of a general phenomenon, and it appears that early first-century Britain may not have been a special case.

BIBLIOGRAPHY

Buchi, E. 1971. 'Banchi di anfore romane a Verona. Note sui commerci Cisalpini', *Il Territorio Veronese in età Romana*, Verona, 531–637.

Deniaux, E. 1980. *Recherches sur les amphores antiques de Basse Normandie*, Caen.

Ettlinger, E. 1977. 'Aspects of amphora typology—seen from the north', *Coll. E.F.R.* xxxii, 9–16.

Galliou, P. 1983. 'Days of wine and roses? Early Armorica and the Atlantic wine trade', this volume.

Hawkes, C. F. C. and Hull, M. R. 1947. *Camulodunum*, Soc. Antiq. London Res. Rep. xiv.

Panella, C. 1973. 'Appunti su un gruppo di anfore della prima, media e tarda età imperiale', *Ostia*, iii, 460–633.

Parker, A. J. 1971. 'The evidence provided by underwater archaeology for Roman trade in the western Mediterranean', in D. J. Blackman (ed.), *Marine Archaeology: Colston Papers*, xxiii, 361–81.

Partridge, C. 1979. 'Excavations at Puckeridge and Braughing 1975–79', *Herts. Arch.* vii, 28–132.

—— 1981. *Skeleton Green*, Britannia Monograph 2, London.

Pascual Guasch, R. 1980. 'La evolución de las exportaciones beticas durante el Imperio', in J. M. Blázquez Martínez (ed.), *Producción y comercio del aceite en la Antigüedad*, Madrid, 233–42.

Peacock, D. P. S. 1971. 'Roman amphorae in pre-Roman Britain', in M. Jesson and D. Hill (eds.), *The Iron Age and its Hillforts*, Southampton, 161–88.

Riley, J. A. 1982. 'The coarse pottery from Berenice', in J. A. Lloyd, *Excavations at Sidi Khrebish Benghazi (Berenice)*, vol. 2, 91–466, Tripoli.

Sanquer, R. 1971. 'Chronique d'archéologie antique et médiévale', *Bull. Soc. arch. Finistère*, xcvii, 19–83.

Tchernia, A. 1983. 'Italian wine in Gaul at the end of the Republic', in P. Garnsey, K. Hopkins and C. R. Whittaker (eds.), *Trade in the Ancient Economy*, London, 87–104.

Wheeler, R. E. M. and Wheeler, T. V. 1936. *Verulamium: a Belgic and Two Roman Cities*, Soc. Antiq. London Res. Rep. xi.

Williams, D. F. 1981. 'Roman amphora trade with Late Iron Age Britain', in H. Howard and E. Morris (eds.), *Production and Distribution: a Ceramic Viewpoint*, B.A.R. S 120, Oxford, 123–32.

Williams, D. F. and Peacock, D. P. S. Forthcoming. 'The importation of olive oil into Iron Age and Roman Britain', *2do Congreso sobre producción y commercio del aceite en la Antigüedad*, Seville 1982.

Some Notes on Imported Metalwork in Iron Age Britain

I. M. Stead, F.S.A.

There has been a tendency sometimes for insular archaeologists to regard any fine or unusual piece of metalwork rather vaguely as an import without considering its position in a European context. This is, of course, a nonsense because in Britain throughout the Iron Age skilled smiths worked iron, bronze and gold to a standard every bit as high as that of their counterparts on the Continent. They produced masterpieces which are outstanding in a European context, such as the Battersea shield, Waterloo helmet and Snettisham torque, and were very capable of supplying all native needs for domestic, industrial and military purposes as well as for show. Some metalwork was certainly imported, but it must have been a rarity: it could have arrived by merchants trading, gifts from abroad, or by visitors or immigrants bringing their personal possessions. Such traffic was not limited to one direction, for some pieces of British manufacture definitely found their way onto the Continent.

At a simple level an import can be defined as a securely provenanced outlying example of a type which is firmly established elsewhere. The cordoned bucket found at Weybridge in 1907 provides a good example, because it is the only piece in Britain of a type well-known in central Europe (pl. I*a*). Its provenance is not immediately convincing, for it is said to have been found below 4 m. of clay and sand in the course of excavating the foundations for a bridge; no archaeologist saw it *in situ* and it was sold to an antiquities collector who lived many miles away (Smith 1908). However, the bridge was over a river, the River Wey, and the bucket could well have come from a former course of the river. Only 100 m. away an Iron Age settlement has since been excavated, producing pottery which might well have been contemporary with the bucket (Hanworth and Tomalin 1977). The settlement is particularly important because it produced evidence of iron-working, and in the immediate vicinity there is a well-known deposit of iron ore which was still

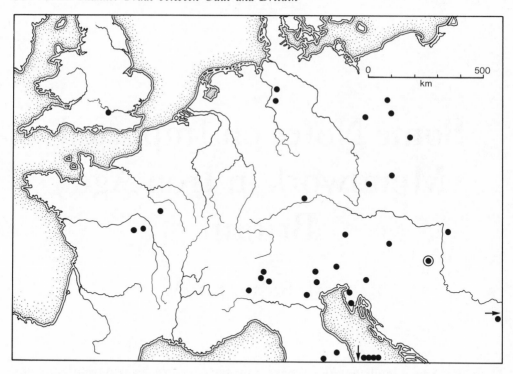

FIG. 16. Distribution of cordoned buckets with swing-handles and nine cordons on the body. The encircled dot is Kurd, where ten such buckets were found

being worked early in the nineteenth century (Sherlock 1962, 58). It is only 3 km. south of the River Thames and in an ideal position for trading and receiving exotic imports. In Europe there are at least 186 cordoned buckets with swing-handles, of which fifty-six resemble Weybridge in having nine cordons on the body (Stjernquist 1967; Bouloumié 1976; Pellet and Delor 1980, 46–7). The Weybridge bucket is markedly an outlyer (fig. 16) and seems to be identical with some of the Continental pieces.

More or less contemporary with the bucket, and apparently found not far away, is a very fine iron sword (fig. 17, 1). Although first published in 1905 (Smith 1905, 95, fig. 72) it was apparently known a decade earlier, because it appears in an illustration prepared by Arthur Evans in 1895 for the Rhind Lectures (Evans 1908, 128, fig. 7). It was certainly in the British Museum by 1905 but was not registered until 1936, when an old label recorded it from the 'Thames at London'. Smith (1905, 95, fig. 72 and 1925, 88, fig. 84) gives its provenance simply as 'Thames'; Evans (1908, 128, fig. 7) adds 'London'. Its excellent patina is certainly consistent with its having been found in the Thames. The sword has been claimed as an import but, unlike the Weybridge bucket, there is no exact parallel on the Continent. Hallstatt C/D iron swords and daggers whose pommels extend outwards in two antennae are found in central and western Europe—there are several varieties and the type was obviously manufactured in different centres (Mariën 1958, 119–21; Kossack 1959; Jope 1961a, 326, 329; Rieth 1969; Schüle 1969; Drack 1973; Wamser 1975; Harrison 1980). Wherever these weapons have

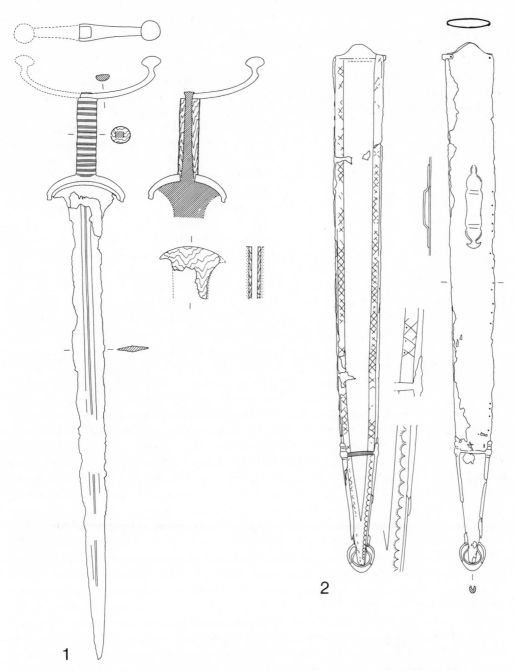

1

2

FIG. 17. 1. Hallstatt iron sword from the Thames, with drawings to illustrate the construction of the hilt and to show the surviving extent of the wooden scabbard-lining; 2. The iron scabbard from Orton Meadows. Scale ¼, with details of the decoration on the scabbard at ½.

been sufficiently well preserved and wherever they have been properly studied the construction of the hilts of both daggers and swords follows a very similar pattern. The Thames piece provides a typical illustration: first the curved hilt-guard was fitted over the tang onto the top of the blade; then the tang was covered by a wooden tube which can be seen through a crack at the top, and its grain is visible on radiographs where the wood has been soaked with iron salts; the wood was encased in iron, with a seam down one side; and finally the antennae pommel was attached and the top of the tang burred over to secure the lot. Of the scabbard all that survives is a thickness of wood whose structure has been replaced by iron salts (pl. I*b*). The top corners seem to flare much more than the shoulders of the blade (although the very edge of the blade cannot be distinguished on radiographs); on one side the wood has laminated and three layers can be distinguished, but all the grain runs in the same direction and there is no sign of a joint at the edge, so it could have been carved from a single piece of wood. The curved mouth of the scabbard is defined by the impression of an edge on top of the wood (fig. 17, pl. I*b*), possibly the impression of a metal reinforcement for the mouth, or even the mouth of a metal scabbard, in which case the wood was a lining, and perhaps a lining only for the mouth of the scabbard. Despite the similarities in hilt construction the Thames sword still seems to lack an exact parallel. Swords with antennae hilts, as opposed to daggers, are quite rare: the Thames example is undoubtedly a sword, with a blade just over 500 mm. long, very similar in length to a much corroded example from Dörflingen, Switzerland (Drack 1973, 128), whilst a longer weapon from Camallera, Spain, is better preserved and apparently more comparable in detail (Schüle 1969, 90, pl. 184, 1). But one detail of the Thames sword deserves comment, for the surviving antenna is exceptionally long: antennae pommels are always longer than the hilt-guards, but usually in the ratio 3:2; for the Thames example the ratio is almost 2:1, which seems unmatched on a Continental sword.

But regardless of whether or not the sword was an import, the same kind of hilt construction was used on an undoubtedly native dagger—or, rather, a dagger in a distinctively British sheath. This Hallstatt D dagger, also found in the Thames, has a straight bar-like pommel and hilt-guard which can be matched in central Europe and France (Jope 1961a, 326, 329). Its sheath is unusual in that it was made of wood wrapped by a series of adjoining or overlapping bronze strips riveted to the wood in a straight line down the back. Four similar sheaths are known, three others from the Thames and one from Belgium (*ibid.*, nos. 1–3; Mariën 1963; Macdonald 1978); although all contain dagger blades only the one has a surviving hilt. Four of the five sheaths, including the one from Belgium, have remains or traces of a distinctively British double suspension-loop instead of the single suspension-loop normally found on the Continent. In this instance the Continental example is the outlyer, and was presumably exported from Britain.

The double suspension-loop serves to distinguish another series of British Hallstatt D and La Tène I short sword-scabbards or dagger-sheaths from their Continental counterparts (Jope 1961a). Judged by their bronze front-plates they could well be taken for imports from Champagne, but the double suspension-loop on the reverse betrays their British manufacture. Chapes in Champagne and southern England developed along similar lines, with projecting anchor-terminals ultimately turned back to the sheath and the tubular chape replaced by the La Tène frame-chape (Jope 1974). Typologically the sheath from West Buckland,

Somerset (Jope 1961a, no. 21), is late, with a La Tène I annular chape-end (unfortunately the upper part has broken away); it illustrates two features common to the series—first, the British double suspension-loop, and second, the geometric ornament (here cross-hatched triangles) which often decorates the borders of the front-plates in England and France (fig. 18).

It has been said that the British tradition of Hallstatt and Early La Tène daggers or short swords came to an end, and was succeeded after a hiatus by a new series of swords influenced by the Continental La Tène II forms (Piggott 1950, 4–5; Jope 1961a, 308, 320). The only well-known exceptions are the Witham and Standlake swords, the latter in a scabbard with a La Tène I open chape-end, but even that has usually been dated late (*ibid.*; de Navarro 1960, 91, n. 25). La Tène I scabbards are indeed rare in Britain, but swords of La Tène I shape are fairly numerous and include at least seventeen from the rivers Thames and Witham. De Navarro was well aware of the British Early La Tène swords, but he published only one—a piece which he regarded as an import (de Navarro 1966). This sword is fragmentary—the tang and the upper part of the blade are missing—and only small fragments of the scabbard are attached. It was found in an old channel of the River Lea during the construction of the Lockwood Reservoir at Walthamstow (Hatley 1933, 19, 29), and its discovery in waterlogged conditions accounts for the excellent condition of the iron. The original surface of the blade is well preserved and its entire length on both sides is covered with closely spaced horizontal lines which are quite sharply defined and have been either engraved or chased (pl. II*b*). This 'laddering' is a very rare feature which is found occasionally on swords and scabbards in Switzerland; apart from the Walthamstow example, de Navarro knew of two La Tène I swords and four scabbards (three La Tène II and one La Tène I) all from Lake Neuchâtel, and one scabbard (probably La Tène II) from Yugoslavia. He also drew attention to a scabbard-plate from Sutton-on-Trent (Fox 1958, pl. 21) whose ornament recalled this tradition, but there the laddering is in panels alternating with more elaborate decoration on a plate of bronze, not iron, which has no close Continental parallel. Another British bronze scabbard with fine close laddering has just come to light (from Wittenham, bought by the Ashmolean Museum at Christie's in October 1982) as the present paper was being completed (pl. II*d*).

De Navarro's list of three swords with 'laddering' can now be doubled. First, there is a fine example on a sword dredged from the River Saône (Chalon-sur-Saône museum, 20.1.1955). Only its lower part survives, and its end is embedded in its scabbard, but the blade has a typical La Tène I taper, a median ridge, and the chape-end is of de Navarro's type Iδ (a La Tène I form). The laddering is on both sides, at intervals of 1.5 mm. to 2 mm., and shows as superficial dark lines presumably formed by a blunt tool. Secondly, laddering has been observed on the surviving part of the blade of the Chatenay-Macheron anthropoid-hilted sword; this one is slightly different from the others because the lines are closely spaced, sharply and finely marked, and it is the only laddered blade which has neither mid-rib nor median ridge (Clarke and Hawkes 1955, 223, no. 27; but the laddering has not been published hitherto, pl. II*c*). The third piece to be added to the list is an excellent and important example recently found in Britain, on a typical La Tène I tapering blade (538 mm. long) which is laddered on both sides wherever the surface survives, right down to the tip. In contrast to the Walthamstow example,

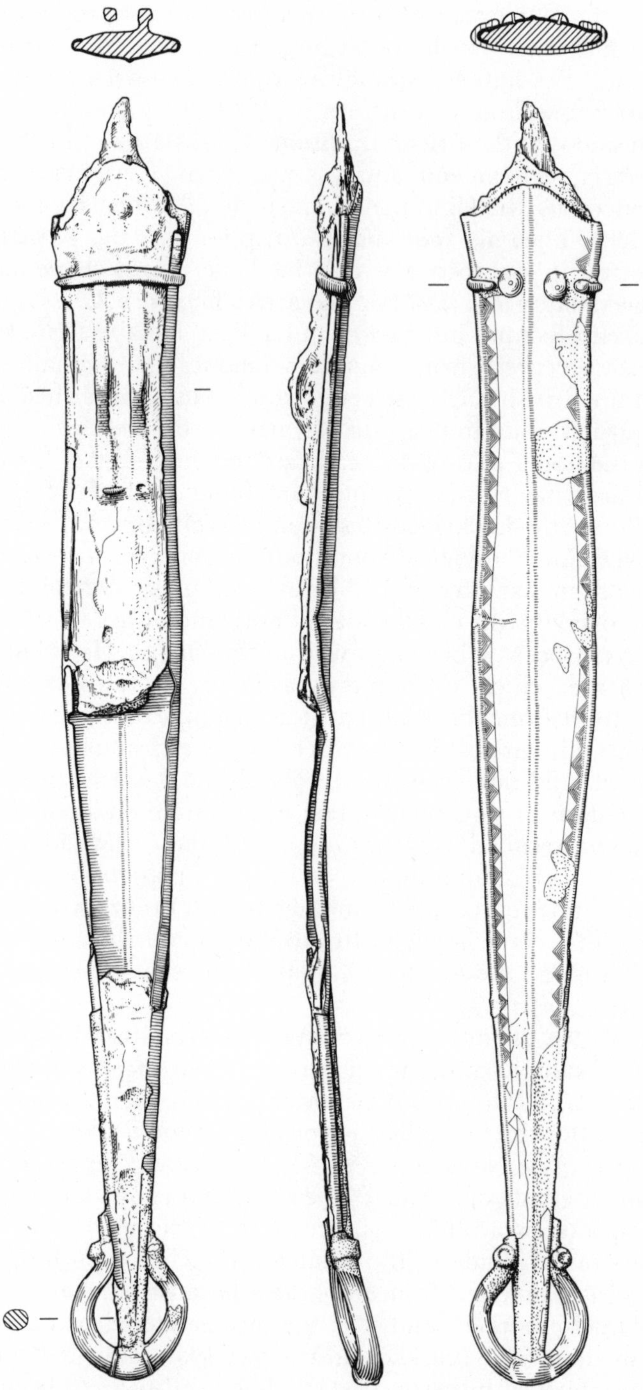

FIG. 18. Remains of an iron dagger in a sheath with bronze front-plate and iron back-plate, from West Buckland. Scale ½

the laddering here is less sharply defined and may have been hammered or punched—it certainly does not seem to have been engraved or chased (pl. II*a*). The new sword comes from Orton Meadows, near Peterborough, where it was discovered with other iron objects in an old course of the River Nene, and it is particularly important because nearly all of the iron scabbard survives. The scabbard is undoubtedly La Tène I, and has features which suggest an early date in La Tène I (fig. 17, 2). Not only has it an open chape-end, but the top of the chape is bridged on both sides, slightly below the top of the binding, by a ribbed strip of iron. This is a form to be contrasted with the typical La Tène chape, which is bridged on the back and clamped on the front, and it can be matched on early pieces from the Continent such as the scabbard from the Somme-Bionne cart burial. The front-plate of the scabbard is decorated down both sides; within the chape there are compass-drawn semicircles bordered by arcs of fine punched dots, whilst above the chape the decoration changes to criss-cross lines forming lozenges and triangles, with punched dots central to the triangles. Such decoration recalls that on dagger-sheaths in England and northern France, but, in contrast to the laddering, it does not have close Swiss connotations. A further detail is typical of neither the Continent nor Britain, for the suspension-loop is not in the expected position at the top of the scabbard, but quite some distance below. A comparable position was used on some much later British scabbards (Piggott 1950, 17–21), and there are rivet-holes in a similar position on an undecorated Irish scabbard from Lisnacroghera (Wood-Martin 1886, 65–6, pl. xII, fig. 1, where the chape has been mounted back to front). The Orton Meadows scabbard is surely British, and the sword may well be native too; they demonstrate continuity from the British Hallstatt D and La Tène I daggers and short swords, and suggest that British armourers may have produced the long sword no later than their Continental colleagues. It is as early as (if not earlier than) any example with laddering from the Continent, and its discovery reduces the chances of the Walthamstow sword having been an import.

Laddering is not the only form of decoration on Swiss swords, which occasionally are decorated with overall punched ornament (Wyss 1968, 668, pl. 3, nos. 1 and 2, from Port). Such ornament is more common on scabbards, where it is known as chagrinage and assumed to be a copy in metal of the surface of a leather scabbard (de Navarro 1972, 104–5). Shagreened scabbards are always of Middle La Tène form and are found mainly in Switzerland. Outside Switzerland shagreened swords are rare, and inevitably found in water; there is one example from the River Saône (Chalon-sur-Saône museum, 54.13.1) and two from the River Thames at Battersea. One of the Battersea swords has triangular punched marks over all but the borders of the blade; it may be a La Tène I piece, certainly it tapers to a sharp point, but the blade is quite flat (pl. II*e*; B.M. 1861.6–20.3). This is probably the piece described by Franks: 'on one of the blades are punctured ornaments similar to those that occur on the Swiss examples' (Franks 1880, 257). The second Battersea sword has a slight but definite median ridge and also tapers to a long sharp point in the La Tène I manner (pl. II*f*; Museum of London, A.13868). The punched impression is small and rather oval, but in places has been struck at an angle which gives it a triangular appearance. Lawrence (1929, 88) mentions that 'a sword blade in the London Museum has hammered indents all down the blade'—presumably this sword from Battersea. It is interesting that both

British swords with chagrinage have the La Tène I taper, whereas in Switzerland both swords and scabbards with chagrinage are La Tène II in date. This does not necessarily mean that the British examples are earlier in date, because in some parts of Europe the tapering blade continued into La Tène II (the East Celtic area: de Navarro 1966, 152; Champagne: Stead 1983), but it does mean that the Battersea swords are unlikely to have been exported from Switzerland.

Another piece from the Thames at Battersea (B.M. 1859.1–22.1) still further illustrates foreign influence on British armourers, because the top of the scabbard is decorated with a dragon-pair (fig. 19, 1: pl. IIIa). Dragon-pairs, and their derivative bird-pairs, are heraldic-like devices which ornament the upper parts of some La Tène I and II scabbards (de Navarro 1972, 216–38). They are found especially in Switzerland and Hungary, although in recent years several have been recorded from France. Dragons with lyre- or S-shaped bodies like the one from Battersea are essentially East Celtic: they were classified by de Navarro as type II and there are now eleven East Celtic examples to compare with two from France, one from Switzerland and one from south Germany (fig. 19, 2; de Navarro 1972, 224–5; Szabó 1974, 248–9; Bulard 1979, 36–8). The stippled background is not common, but occurs twice with Hungarian dragon-pairs (de Navarro 1972, 223) and once with a French example (Bulard 1979, fig. 2, no. 1). The British piece is very closely linked to this Continental tradition, but as yet it cannot be matched exactly; in particular, the scabbard-mouth is very low, and dragon-pairs usually ornament scabbards with mid-ribs or median ridges. A second piece from the Thames has traces of stippled ornament in this position—it too may have a dragon-pair, but it awaits conservation treatment. Derivatives of dragon-pairs were to have quite a history in Britain, although few examples survive. The earliest, typologically, is on a newly discovered scabbard from Fovant in Wiltshire (fig. 19, 3; Salisbury Museum). Although a long way from the prototype, it has a confronted design in which features such as the tail (cf. type I and III dragon-pairs) and the beaks or lips can still be distinguished.

Laddering, chagrinage and dragon-pairs all show that British armourers were in touch with Continental practices, but only two examples—the laddered sword from Walthamstow and the dragon-pair from Battersea—can be considered as possible imports.

Brooches present rather different problems. There are so many of them with a superficial similarity across the La Tène world and then the Roman provinces, and they tend to be studied on a regional or national basis. Detailed international studies of specific types aimed at establishing local workshops are lacking. As far as Britain is concerned a great deal of research is in progress, or awaiting publication, and the published material is very scattered. M. R. Hull's corpus of Iron Age and Romano-British brooches is being edited for publication by C. F. C. Hawkes and M. G. Simpson; A. C. H. Olivier's research on La Tène III brooches is nearing completion; a useful thesis on La Tène I brooches by A. M. Wardman remains unpublished; and there are large collections of La Tène brooches from the recent excavations at Burton Fleming and Wetwang Slack, North Humberside. The only full treatment of la Tène I brooches appeared fifty-seven years ago (Fox 1927). But brooches are one of the most significant metal artefacts and they cannot be ignored in any consideration of imports.

One of the earliest La Tène types to be found in Britain is the so-called

FIG. 19. Dragon-pair ornament on iron scabbards: 1. River Thames at Battersea; 2. Taliándörögd (after de Navarro 1972, pl. CXXIX, 3). Ornament derived from dragon-pairs on iron scabbards; 3. Fovant; 4. Bonyhádvarasd (after *ibid.*, pl. CLII, 2). Scale $\frac{1}{1}$

Marzabotto brooch (ApSimon 1959, 'Hammersmith' type; Wardman 1972, 'Box' type). It takes its name from an atypical example in an Italian cemetery; rare in Italy but popular north of the Alps, its *floruit* was probably before the Celts reached Italy *c.* 390 B.C. (Kruta 1979, 82). There has been no detailed study to establish regional variations, but some British examples clearly stand apart because of the way in which the spring was constructed. An example in the British Museum (B.M. 1927.12–12.8; fig. 20, 1) has a bow neatly ribbed on each side of a slight

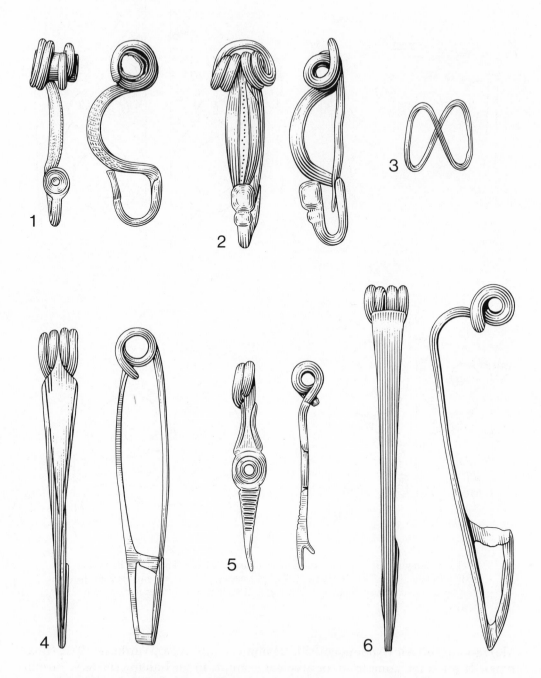

FIG. 20. Bronze brooches: 1. ?Suffolk; 2. Blandford; 4. Hockwold; 5. Blandford; 6. Aylesford. 3. Silver finger-ring from Park Brow. Scale $\frac{1}{1}$

central groove (very worn on top), and a foot terminating in a dished circular setting for a piece of inlay. It has all the proportions of a Continental brooch, but its 'spring' is the remains of a hinged device and not a true spring. It was made in three parts: two coils in one with the bow, two coils with the pin, and a hollow bronze cylindrical rivet linking the other two pieces through the four coils. The pin and part of its adjoining coil is now missing. The outer coils have been neatly filed flat, and there has never been any form of a chord. This brooch was acquired via G. F. Lawrence from the sale of, mainly, Suffolk antiquities belonging to S. G. Fenton (lot 147, Sotheby's, 28th November 1927); the museum register records 'probably Lakenheath' on the authority of Lawrence; Clarke (1939, 33, 98 and fig. 6, no. 4) is more cautious: 'locality unknown—perhaps from north-west part of [Suffolk]'. Marzabotto brooches from Cowlam (Stead 1979, 64), Danebury (Cunliffe 1971, 243, described by Wardman 1972, 20) and Hammersmith (Fox 1927, no. 51; Hodson 1971, 55; described by Wardman 1972, 15–16) and a variety from Burton Fleming (Stead 1979, 94) all have (or have had) hinged pins and are thus unlike any example from the Continent. On the other hand, most Marzabotto brooches from Britain have true springs—those from Box and Islip are good examples (Fox 1927, nos. 10 and 22)—and amongst them there could be an import. The arrival of the type in Britain is doubtless explained by the importation of a Continental example, but the case for regarding any of the surviving pieces as an import has yet to be proved.

One distinctively British brooch, the Blandford type (Hodson 1964, 137; Fowler 1953, type 1a; Wardman 1972, Wessex type), shows that British craftsmen continued to make some La Tène I brooches with true springs. This local type has a distribution centred on Wessex, and is characterized by a four-coiled spring with external chord, a rounded foot with a rather heavy element, and a bow which often has a row of punched dots along its length. Whilst several examples have hinged pins, the brooch from Blandford itself (fig. 20, 2) and some others certainly have true springs.

The two Dux brooches from Wallingford in Berkshire (one a classic form with internal chord and the other, with external chord, of a type well represented at Dux) rank among the best-known imports in Britain; almost certainly they are Continental brooches, so their provenance warrants close investigation. They were originally published along with fifteen others, ranging from Hallstatt Italian forms to late Roman cross-bow brooches, as a collection which conveniently traced the history of the Iron Age and Roman brooch (Page and Calthrop 1906, 222–7). Three of the specimens were said to have been found at Reading, but the others, including the 'Wallingford' brooches, were unprovenanced. The collection 'was bequeathed to the [Reading] museum by Mr. Davies of Wallingford, who for many years was known to be a collector of local antiquities, and often secured specimens from labourers and others in his neighbourhood. *It is conceivable that some were obtained from the Continent*' (*ibid.*, 223; my italics). In fact, a glance at the illustrations suggests very strongly that some were obtained from the Continent. Of the Roman pieces, apart from two cross-bow brooches, there is no common Romano-British type—no Colchester, dolphin, Hod Hill or trumpet brooch. Instead there is one clear Pannonian brooch and a number of others common along the Danube but rare along the Thames. It is a collection which could have been acquired from a London dealer with a contact in Vienna. Although the original publication left these brooches unprovenanced, only two years later Goddard (1908, 401) firmly ascribed them to Wallingford, and subsequent writers have followed him. Even if Davies had given a local provenance to his Dux brooches there would have been some doubt about them: of the coins in his collection 'an unusually high proportion had local provenances' and it is suspected that he was 'supplied with coins by persons who gave spurious provenances to pieces which they hoped to sell to him' (Metcalf 1980, 48). Peake (1931, 65) dismisses two Hallstatt brooches said to have been found near Wallingford because 'they were obtained from a collector (Davies), who made his purchases without a too critical inquiry into their source'; he makes no mention of the Dux brooches, presumably for the same reason. It seems very unlikely that the Dux brooches were found at Wallingford; unlikely that they were found in Britain; and it is even possible that they came from Dux itself. The Dux hoard consisted of a cauldron and probably about 2,000 bronze objects, mainly brooches and bracelets (Kruta 1971). It was discovered in January 1882, and the exact number of objects is unknown because many of the pieces were quickly dispersed and snapped up by private collectors. In view of the inter-national trade in antiquities it is quite conceivable that Davies acquired the two brooches from this source; the earliest record of his brooches is in November 1883 (almost two years after the Dux discovery) when they were deposited on loan at Reading Museum.

Dux brooches were certainly on the London market by 1891, following the sale of no less than thirty-two from the Egger Collection at Sotheby's on 25th June 1891 (lots 130, 131 and 228–30). Not one of these can be traced with certainty, but their presence in Britain means that the provenance of any Dux-type brooch acquired subsequent to 1891 must be examined critically. In particular, there are three classic Dux-type brooches and one related piece in the Museum of London: Fox (1927, no. 50, and p. 109, n. 3) listed one (A.11927, 'R. Thames, probably at Kingston') and referred to the others (A.21465, A.22304 and A.22357) with the comment that 'the evidence [of provenance] is not exact enough to permit inclusion in this list'. How Fox obtained his Kingston provenance is not known, for the museum register lists all from the Thames, three 'near London' and the other 'probably at London'; one was bought in 1913 and three in 1920. Jean Macdonald considers that a sale-room source is only too likely, especially in view of the vague provenance, which she contrasts with that of an undoubtedly native Blandford-type brooch (Fox 1927, no. 49) acquired about the same time, where the register gives 'found in the Thames at Mortlake, November 6th 1917. Bought November 1917'. On the other hand she comments on the sound dark brown patina—'compatible enough with genuine Thames finds'. A brooch undoubtedly from Dux acquired by the British Museum in 1902 does not have a sound river patina, nor does an unprovenanced Dux-type brooch bought by the same museum in 1911.

Many British La Tène II and III brooches were produced locally, and the involuted series developed quite independently of Continental traditions. But Continental influence made itself felt in La Tène III, for there are certainly five and possibly seven Nauheim brooches in England. The example illustrated (fig. 20, 4), excavated by Charles Green at Hockwold, Norfolk, could well be taken for a Continental brooch. Rather surprisingly there is also a British example of the Cenisola variety of Nauheim brooch. This variety also has a four-coil spring with internal chord, and an open catch-plate, but it differs in having a central circular

PLATE I 55

a. The Weybridge bucket. Height (excluding handle-mounts) 180 mm.

b. Hallstatt iron sword from the River Thames, showing traces of the wooden scabbard-lining (approx. full size)

Photographs: British Museum

Laddering on sword blades from: *a*. Orton Meadows; *b*. Walthamstow; *c*. Chatenay-Macheron. *d*. Laddering on a bronze scabbard from Wittenham. *e–f*. Chagrinage on sword blades from the River Thames at Battersea. Scale approx. full size

Photographs: a–e, British Museum; f, Museum of London

PLATE III   57

a

b

c

d

a. Dragon-pair on an iron scabbard from the River Thames at Battersea. *b–c*. Brooches from the Le Catillon hoard, in a private collection in Australia. *d*. The Aylesford bucket, showing vertical divisions between the panels of repoussé ornament. *a–c* are approx. full size

Photographs: a, d, British Museum; b–c, R. K. Harding, University of Sydney

The new reconstruction of the Aylesford bucket. Height (excluding handle-mounts)
300 mm

Photograph: British Museum

motif on the bow (fig. 20, 5). It is a rare variety whose distribution is concentrated immediately south of the Alps (Werner 1955, 186 and map p. 194); to Werner's sole example north of the Alps (Karlstein) may be added Besançon (Lerat 1956, 10, no. 68) and Altenburg-Rheinau (Fischer 1966, 296, fig. 2, no. 3). The British brooch differs from published Continental examples in having a narrower head and a perforated disc, but undoubtedly it belongs to this type. It is said to be from Blandford, Dorset, and came to the British Museum with a large collection of antiquities formed by Henry Durden. Most antiquities in the Durden Collection are local, and there is no reason to suppose that recorded provenances are unreliable; amongst the brooches the only obvious query is an Italian Hallstatt brooch, but that, unlike the Cenisola variety, is unprovenanced.

There are several other British pieces related to the Nauheim brooch, including a series with external chords, and it is obvious that the native brooch industry was still flourishing. A good example of a British variety is a recent discovery from the Aylesford cemetery (fig. 20, 6)—a brooch found in a cinerary urn excavated in 1886 but not emptied until almost a century later (registered as 88.10–24.40, found in the pot 88.10–24.15, i.e. Birchall 1965, 304, no. 75). This brooch resembles the Nauheim in construction, but its bow is too thick and it rises too sharply at the head.

Another La Tène III brooch (B.M. 1907.10–24.2), a really fine specimen, has parallels in the same south Alpine region as the Cenisola variety (Fox 1958, pl. 40A, 'from River Thames'). But it was registered with a number of objects 'from drawers and cupboards without further information' and the comment in the register, 'possibly from Thames', is doubtless a guess based on its excellent patina. Ettlinger (1973, 51) is right to reject its English provenance.

Far more convincing as candidates for imports are the two pairs of *Knotenfibeln* from Great Chesterford, claimed by Krämer (1971, 124–7) as exported from Italy. The claim rests not only on the form of the brooches but on the metal from which they were produced—because they are made of silver. The Great Chesterford brooches may be compared with examples from Folkestone (Stead 1976, 406, fig. 2, no. 6) and the Le Catillon hoard (Krämer 1971, fig. 4, no. 4). Krämer published three brooches from the Le Catillon hoard, two of bronze and one of silver. The silver brooch had part of a silver chain attached and there was also a separate length of silver brooch-chain. Unfortunately these brooches were stolen from the museum at St. Helier, and Krämer's drawings were taken from photographs. Curiously, two other brooches exist: it seems that they were separated from the rest of the hoard at a very early stage and are now in a private collection in Australia; J. V. S. Megaw has photographs of them (pl. III*b* and *c*). One is complete, has a length of brooch-chain attached, seems to be identical to the silver brooch (*ibid.*; fig. 4, no. 4) and is almost certainly its pair and presumably also made of silver. The second brooch, lacking the foot and part of the pin, is comparable with Krämer's fig. 4, nos. 3 and 5 (judging from the proportions it could be the pair to no. 3) which are said to be bronze. The complete (unpublished) Le Catillon 'silver' brooch has a catch-plate divided in a way very similar to that of the only complete Great Chesterford brooch; the Le Catillon pair differs in having a hook adjoining the moulding on the bow, and in this respect the broken Folkestone brooch more closely resembles those from Great Chesterford. All seven silver brooches have two-coil springs and external chords; a closely related pair from Faversham (Stead 1976, 406, fig. 3, no. 1) has four-coil springs and internal chords and there is another silver brooch of this type from Folkestone (*ibid.*, fig. 2, no. 5). Ten very similar brooches from the British Isles would normally be regarded as local products, but the use of silver argues for caution (for a report on the composition of two of the brooches, see p. 64). Brooches made of precious metals are rare in the La Tène world, and the occasional silver and even gold specimens north of the Alps are far outnumbered by examples from Italy (Krämer 1971). As imports from Italy in the years after the Caesarian expeditions silver brooches would not be alone, because wine amphorae were certainly being imported (pp. 37–42) and the silver wine cups from Welwyn and Welwyn Garden City are surely Italian (Strong 1967).

If these silver brooches were indeed imports, then they form the largest group of brooches imported into Britain before the birth of Christ. The Le Catillon examples came from a hoard, and the others are certainly or probably from burials. Examples of deliberate burial, in Britain restricted to the graves of the Arras and Aylesford cultures, obviously give an unbalanced picture of the numbers and distribution of brooches (Stead 1979, 89–90); for most of the British Iron Age surviving examples are chance finds of casual losses and must represent a very small percentage of the brooches manufactured. Although there is scarcely a hint of this flourishing industry from unfinished specimens or discarded moulds, it seems clear that most La Tène brooches found in Britain were also produced in Britain. The same is probably true of Romano-British brooches after the Claudian conquest, but for the half century before the conquest most authorities seem to favour a high proportion of imports. A detailed study of specific types in Britain and on the Continent is needed to support or refute this contention.

Swords and brooches have been dealt with in some detail, though by no means exhaustively, but the rest of the paper is much more selective, dealing with a few famous objects which some scholars have accepted as imports.

The small bronze figurine from Aust (Fox 1958, pl. 2F) has sometimes been claimed as an import from Spain. It was found by a Mr. James Spratt at 'the base of Aust Cliff, in a position indicating its recent fall with a heap of debris which lay near, from the ever-crumbling rock above it' (Ellis 1900). This happened in August 1900, and the figurine was promptly bought by the British Museum for a sovereign, which was perhaps rather a high price for a unique object found under those circumstances. However, following a recent examination by the British Museum Research Laboratory, it was reported that details of the corrosion suggested 'very strongly that the figure is of considerable antiquity'. Its sole surviving glass eye is a little unusual in composition—a potash glass with manganese as a decolourant—but this is not completely unknown from the first millennium B.C. Certainly the figurine is an authentic antiquity, but it is very unlikely that it came from Spain. The head-dress bears a certain resemblance to those on some Spanish figurines, but beyond that there is no comparison—an opinion that can be stated with confidence because it is held by Gérard Nicolini, the foremost authority on Spanish figurines. In the absence of Continental parallels the Aust figurine must be accepted as British.

Unlike the Aust figurine, the Aylesford bucket has a very reasonable provenance and can be seen clearly in a European context. It was examined in detail in 1969, following the discovery of a pair of comparable buckets at Baldock, and a new reconstruction was suggested (Stead 1971). That reconstruction has now been completed (pl. IV), and the most significant change is the addition of three feet. Of the plaques now facing the feet, part of one only is original—an important fragment which had been omitted from the previous reconstruction because it had two clear edges at right-angles to one another and could never have belonged to the decorative band at the top. The loss of the rest of the bronze facing is not surprising, because the feet of such vessels would have been very vulnerable to damage and decay; the Aylesford bucket may well have been quite old when placed in the grave, and certainly it had been repaired more than once. It has been shown that the head A2 had been riveted to the bucket on two occasions, leaving slightly different rivet-holes in the bronze bands (*ibid.*, 264). It was ultimately attached by solder to the piece B1 which was in turn riveted to the bucket (this corrects *ibid.*, 264, where it was said that mastic had been used: the British Museum Research Laboratory has confirmed the presence of solder). When the second head, A1, was removed from the old reconstruction in 1980 it was seen that it too had been three times attached to the bucket, on each occasion creating new rivet-holes in the bronze bands. The new reconstruction is not entirely satisfactory because the spacing of the bands is unknown. Furthermore, the central band is composed of six fragments joined by modern sheet-bronze soldered on the inside. Of the joins, certainly two and probably three seem genuine, but there is no evidence for the other three; as that band lacks both overlap and pin-holes it seems unlikely to be complete and possible that some of the joins were recently fabricated.

However, the Aylesford bucket was certainly a tripod vessel, and it may be compared with five others found on three sites in the space of only nine years (1966–74—Baldock, two: *ibid.*, 251–60; Goeblingen-Nospelt grave 'B', two: Thill 1967, 92–3; Vieille-Toulouse: Vidal 1976). As a result of the recent finds another nineteenth-century discovery, from Geisenheim, has also been newly reconstructed and provided with three feet (Polenz 1977). These buckets are all of the same general type, but no two sites have produced exactly comparable examples, which is interesting because the Aylesford bucket could well have been mass-produced. There are three decorative motifs in the top band, one of which appears twice whilst the other two occur four times; the fragment from the foot is a repeat of one of the same motifs. Each time the motifs are exactly replicated, so they must have been shaped on 'formers' of bronze or iron. The technique is illustrated by contemporary bronze formers from Santon Downham (Spratling 1970, 190) and an unstratified iron example from Wroxeter (Atkinson 1942, 216–18). On the Aylesford bucket the occasional vertical line (pl. III*d*) may be the impression of the edge of a former. Hence there is a fair chance that more than one bucket was made to this same design, but until another is found it must be assumed that this one was made not too far away from where it was buried.

Although the Aylesford bucket may well have been native, the bronze pan and jug found with it were certainly imported (Werner 1978, list II, no. 9, list III, no. 11), and the same is true of similar pieces from graves at Welwyn (*ibid.*, list II, nos. 10 and 11, list III, no. 12). But there are two other Aylesford pans in Britain, both allegedly from London. One (Eggers 1966, 95–6; B.M. 1885.8–4.23) was acquired with three other bronze vessels from the sale of William Chaffers's collection (Sotheby's, 12th June 1855, lot 212). In the sale catalogue they are said to have been 'found in Creed Lane', and two of them, including the Aylesford pan, have labels to that effect (adding '1843'); the register records 'found in Creed Lane,

London, 1843'. Whilst the possibility of a hoard, or a rich burial, cannot be entirely dismissed, it must be emphasized that Chaffers collected from far and wide and had several Mediterranean objects with spurious London provenances (Marsh 1979, 127). The other Aylesford pan, now in Bedford Museum, is labelled simply 'London' and has no further history (Kennett 1972). It would be unwise to place any reliance on these provenances.

One of the most striking examples of a La Tène import in Britain is the bent silver finger-ring from Park Brow, Sussex (fig. 20, 3; B.M. 1926.3–13.12; for a report on its composition see p. 64). Reginald Smith recognized it as an import as soon as it was discovered, and identified its homeland as Switzerland. No other such ring has been found in England and it is undoubtedly an import, if not from Switzerland then from an equally, or more, distant source. But the Park Brow finger-ring is still more unusual because it was found on a domestic site; it had not been deliberately buried in a hoard or a grave, but was lost by chance on a settlement and actually recovered under the controlled conditions of an archaeological excavation. An association between domestic pottery and imported metal-work is too good to be true; incredibly, it would seem that the excavators failed to record its context. The associated pottery is unknown; the feature in which the ring was found is also unknown; indeed the very site is unknown! Three settlements were excavated at Park Brow in the 1920s (plan, Wolseley *et al.* 1927, fig. A): (i) 'Late Bronze Age'; (ii) 'Hallstatt—La Tène I' (= Hawkes 1939, 230, 'Park Brow I'); (iii) 'Romano-British' (which proved to be pre-Roman as well and = Hawkes's 'Park Brow II'). The ring is not mentioned in the accounts written by the excavators, but is described by Smith in a general section on the finds (in Wolseley *et al.* 1927, 20) in which its context is not mentioned. A decade later Hawkes (1939, 231) interpreted Smith's discussion of the ring and pedestalled pots as meaning that it came from Park Brow I; but recently (in letters, June and July 1982) he has reconsidered the matter and now believes that on chronological grounds it must have been found at Park Brow II. Sadly, this excavated import has to be treated as an unassociated stray find.

The final object for this paper is the Brentford horn-cap (Megaw 1970, no. 130), or the so-called Brentford so-called horn-cap. This magnificent piece was in the collection of Thomas Layton (d. 1911) of Brentford. In the Layton Collection catalogue it is listed with 'no locality recorded', and in its initial publication (Smith 1918, 22) no provenance is mentioned. Vulliamy (1930, 129) says that it is '(presumably) from the river', and elsewhere records: 'we are informed that the dredgermen and others who brought antiquities to Mr Layton were in the habit of telling him that they were found near Brentford, believing that he would thus be more readily disposed to buy them; while in reality, they frequently came from other, and sometimes from distant, places' (*ibid.*, 131). Leeds (1933, 58) dropped Vulliamy's '(presumably)' and described it as 'from the Thames in the Layton Collection in Brentford Public Library', and in the caption to his illustration it was simply 'R. Thames, Brentford'—a provenance which henceforth became firmly attached. It has sometimes been regarded as an import, mainly on the basis of its decoration: de Navarro (1952, 73) thought it an excellent example of Jacobsthal's Waldalgesheim Style and suggested that it came from the Middle Rhenish area; in spite of Jope (1961b, 78), who regarded it as much later, de Navarro (1972, 275) continued to see it as Waldalgesheim ornament; Duval (1971, 1973) placed it early in the third century B.C. at the start of his 'free graphic style' (which corresponds to Jacobsthal's Waldalgesheim Style); whilst Frey and Megaw (1976, 54–5) thought it was an insular piece dating no earlier than the middle of the third century B.C. and perhaps even later. Here no attempt will be made to discuss the art style or the date of the piece; attention is concentrated on the class of object, which is well represented in southern England. 'Horn-caps' were listed by Fox (1946, 77), who located twelve examples, to which Spratling (1972, nos. 121, 126–8 and 135) has added five, including two small fragments found on excavations. These objects are cylindrical castings with a solid (or closed) disc-shaped head and a rather smaller collar near the base (Fox 1958, pl. 3). There is sometimes a pin or pin-holes through the hollow shaft, and occasionally wood remains have been found on the inside, so the object was a decorative terminal on a wooden shank. The interpretation of function has never strayed far from a chariot: axle-end, hand-hold or yoke-terminal. But all these functions demand that the type should occur in pairs, and no pairs have ever been found. It would appear that two 'horn-caps' were found together at Ham Hill on two different occasions in the first half of the nineteenth century (*ibid.*, nos. 124–7), but they do not seem to have been pairs. If the 'horn-cap' occupied a unique position on a chariot then it could have been a pole-terminal (*ibid.*, 79, MS. addition), but is there any reason why the function should be limited to chariots or harness? 'Horn-caps' have no close Continental parallels and have never been found in vehicle burials (Stead 1965, 261–2). Those from Ham Hill and Llyn Cerrig Bach were found with vehicle fittings, but also with other kinds of object. The 'horn-cap' is definitely a native type and, apart from Llyn Cerrig Bach, all seventeen examples were found in southern England. It is most unlikely that the 'Brentford' example was an import. As for function, perhaps it could have been a mace-head.

In conclusion, it may seem that this paper has been rather negative and sceptical, in destroying imports rather than creating them. But it must be emphasized that only a very small sample of Iron Age metalwork is available for study (Spratling 1979, 149). Very few imports can be identified, but the similarity of many British pieces to Continental material hints at the presence of imports which have not survived or which still await discovery. It is worth making one final point: there could have been much more imported metal than is here appreciated, even in the small surviving sample; one could be failing to see the wood for the trees. Caesar (*B.G.* v, 2) in his description of Britain noted that 'tin is found inland, and small quantities of iron near the coast; the copper that they use is imported'.

Acknowledgements

This paper has benefited in particular from the stimulating criticism of Christopher Hawkes, F.S.A. and the help and advice of Jean Macdonald, F.S.A. The following colleagues also generously gave of their time and expertise to further the research: Louis Bonnamour, George Boon, F.S.A., Clare Conybeare, Leslie Cram, Simon Dove, Barbara Green, F.S.A., Don Mackreth, F.S.A., Geoff Marsh, Vincent Megaw, F.S.A., Gérard Nicolini, Adrian Olivier, Valery Rigby, Peter Shorer and Mansel Spratling, F.S.A. The line drawings are by Robert Pengelly.

Appendix

Report on the composition of three items of Iron Age jewellery
By P. T. Craddock, F.S.A. (British Museum Research Laboratory)

The three pieces, a brooch from Folkestone (91.3–20.18), a brooch from Faversham (1090.70) and a ring from Park Brow (1926.3–13.12), all described as being of silver, were qualitatively surface-analysed by X-ray fluorescence to check their composition.

All three are indeed basically of silver. The Folkestone brooch was of the highest purity with a little copper and substantial traces of gold and lead. Bromine was also detected, which can be explained by the fact that silver bromide is a stable corrosion product and is quite frequently encountered in the surface patina of ancient silver. The Faversham brooch has several per cent of copper and traces of lead, whilst the Park Brow ring is quite base silver with more than 10 per cent of copper. There are some areas of green corrosion on the surface, and these contain zinc. This suggests that the corrosion has been treated by electro-chemical reduction, which involves the use of zinc and caustic soda, at some time since excavation.

BIBLIOGRAPHY

ApSimon, A. M. 1959. 'The bronze brooches' and 'Notes on the Hammersmith type of La Tène I brooch', in P. A. Rahtz and J. Clevedon Brown, 'Blaise Castle Hill, Bristol, 1957', *University of Bristol, Proc. Spelaeological Soc.* viii, 159–60, 164–8.

Atkinson, D. 1942. *Report on Excavations at Wroxeter, 1923–1927*, Oxford.

Birchall, A. 1965. 'The Aylesford-Swarling culture: the problem of the Belgae reconsidered', *P.P.S.* xxxi, 241–367.

Bouloumié, B. 1976. 'Les cistes à cordons trouvées en Gaule (Belgique, France, Suisse)', *Gallia*, xxxiv, 1–30.

Bulard, A. 1979. 'Fourreaux ornés d'animaux fantastiques affrontés découverts en France', *Etudes Celtiques*, xvi, 27–52.

Clarke, R. R. 1939. 'The Iron Age in Norfolk and Suffolk', *Arch. J.* xcvi, 1–113.

Clarke, R. R. and Hawkes, C. F. C. 1955. 'An iron anthropoid sword from Shouldham, Norfolk, with related Continental and British weapons', *P.P.S.* xxi, 198–227.

Cunliffe, B. W. 1971. 'Danebury, Hampshire: first interim report on the excavation, 1969–70', *Antiq. J.* li, 240–52.

de Navarro, J. M. 1952. 'The Celts in Britain and their art', in M. P. Charlesworth *et al.*, *The Heritage of Early Britain*, London.

—— 1960. 'Zu einigen Schwertscheiden aus La Tène', *Ber. R.G.K.* xl, 79–119.

—— 1966. 'Swords and scabbards of the La Tène period with incised laddering', in R. Degen *et al.* (eds.), *Helvetia Antiqua*, Zurich.

—— 1972. *The Finds from the Site of La Tène, I: Scabbards and the Swords Found in Them*, London.

Drack, W. 1973. 'Waffen und Messer der Hallstattzeit aus dem schweizerischen Mittelland und Jura', *Jahrb. Schweiz. Gesellschaft für Ur- und Frühgeschichte*, lvii, 119–68.

Duval, P.-M. 1971. 'Les styles de l'art celtique occidental: terminologie et chronologie', in J. Filip (ed.), *Actes du VIIe Congrès International des Sciences Préhistoriques et Protohistoriques*, Prague, 1966, vol. 2, 812–17.

—— 1973. 'L'ornement de char de Brentford', in P.-M. Duval (ed.), *Recherches d'archéologie celtique et gallo-romaine*, Geneva.

Eggers, H. J. 1966. 'Römische Bronzegefässe in Britannien', *Jahrb. R.G.Z. Mainz*, xiii, 67–164.

Ellis, F. 1900. 'An ancient bronze figure from Aust Cliff, Gloucestershire', *Trans. Bristol & Glos. Arch. Soc.* xxiii, 323–5.

Ettlinger, E. 1973. *Die römischen Fibeln in der Schweiz*, Bern.

Evans, A. J. 1908. (Untitled paper on Bronze Age chronology) *Proc. Soc. Antiq. London*, 2nd ser. xxii, 121–8.

Fischer, F. 1966. 'Das Oppidum von Altenburg-Rheinau', *Germania*, xliv, 286–312.

Fowler, M. J. 1953. 'The typology of brooches of the Iron Age in Wessex', *Arch. J.* cx, 88–105.

Fox, C. 1927. 'A La Tène I brooch from Wales: with notes on the typology and distribution of these brooches in Britain', *Arch. Camb.* lxxxii, 67–112.

—— 1946. *A Find of the Early Iron Age from Llyn Cerrig Bach, Anglesey*, Cardiff.

—— 1958. *Pattern and Purpose: a Survey of Early Celtic Art in Britain*, Cardiff.

Franks, A. W. 1880. 'Notes on a sword found in Catterdale, Yorkshire, exhibited by Lord Wharncliffe, and on other examples of the same kind', *Archaeologia*, xlv, 251–66.

Frey, O.-H. and Megaw, J. V. S. 1976. 'Palmette and circle: Early Celtic art in Britain and its Continental background', *P.P.S.* xlii, 47–65.

Goddard, E. H. 1908. 'Notes on objects of "Late Celtic" character found in Wiltshire', *Wilts. Arch. Mag.* xxxv, 389–407.

Hanworth, R. and Tomalin, D. J. 1977. *Brooklands, Weybridge: the Excavation of an Iron Age and Medieval Site 1964–5 and 1970–71*, Surrey Arch. Soc. Research Vol. 4.

Harrison, R. J. 1980. 'A tin-plated dagger of the Early Iron Age from Spain', *Madrider Mitteilungen*, xxi, 140–46.

Hatley, A. R. 1933. *Early Days in the Walthamstow District*, Walthamstow Antiq. Soc. Official Publication, 28.

Hawkes, C. F. C. 1939. 'The Caburn pottery and its implications', *Sussex Arch. Coll.* lxxx, 217–62.

Hodson, F. R. 1964. 'La Tène chronology, Continental and British', *Bull. Inst. Arch. London*, iv, 123–41.

—— 1971. 'Three Iron Age brooches from Hammersmith', *B. M. Quarterly*, xxxv, 88–105.

Jope, E. M. 1961a. 'Daggers of the Early Iron Age in Britain', *P.P.S.* xxvii, 307–43.

—— 1961b. 'The beginnings of La Tène ornamental style in the British Isles', in S. S. Frere (ed.), *Problems of the Iron Age in Southern Britain*, London.

—— 1974. 'Iron Age dagger and sword chape construction: technology, taxonomy and prehistory', *Irish Arch. Research Forum*, i, 1–8.

Kennett, D. H. 1972. 'An early Roman skillet in Bedford Museum', *Beds. Arch. J.* vii, 82–3.

Kossack, G. 1959. *Südbayern während der Hallstattzeit*, Römisch-Germanische Forschungen, 24.

Krämer, W. 1971. 'Silberne Fibelpaare aus dem letzten vorchristlichen Jahrhundert', *Germania*, xlix, 111–32.

Kruta, V. 1971. *Le trésor de Duchcov*, Ústí nad Labem.

—— 1979. 'Duchcov-Münsingen: nature et diffusion d'une phase laténienne', in P.-M. Duval and V. Kruta (eds.), *Les mouvements celtiques du Ve au Ier siècle avant notre ère*, Paris.

Lawrence, G. F. 1929. 'Antiquities from the Middle Thames', *Arch. J.* lxxxvi, 69–98.

Leeds, E. T. 1933. *Celtic Ornament in the British Isles down to A.D. 700*, Oxford.

Lerat, L. 1956. *Les fibules gallo-romaines*, Catalogue des collections archéologiques de Besançon, ii, Annales Littéraires de l'Université de Besançon, iii, fasc. 1.

Macdonald, J. 1978. 'An Iron Age dagger in the Royal Ontario Museum', in J. Bird, H. Chapman and J. Clark (eds.), *Collectanea Londiniensia*, London & Middlesex Arch. Soc. Special Paper, no. 2.

Mariën, M.-E. 1958. *Trouvailles du Champ d'Urnes et des tombelles hallstattiennes de Court-St.-Etienne*, Brussels.

—— 1963. 'Poignard hallstattien trouvé à Luttre (Hainaut, Belgique)', in S. Genovés (ed.), *A Pedro Bosch-Gimpera . . .*, Mexico, Instituto Nacional, 307–11.

Marsh, G. 1979. 'Nineteenth and twentieth century antiquities dealers and Arretine ware from London', *Trans. London & Middlesex Arch. Soc.* xxx, 125–9.

Megaw, J. V. S. 1970. *Art of the European Iron Age*, Bath.

Metcalf, D. M. 1980. 'Continuity and change in English monetary history *c.* 973–1086', *Brit. Num. J.* l, 20–49.

Page, W. and Calthrop, C. M. 1906. 'Romano-British Berkshire', in V.C.H., *Berkshire*, i, 197–227.

Peake, H. 1931. *The Archaeology of Berkshire*, London.

Pellet, C. and Delor, J.-P. 1980. 'Les ensembles funéraires de "la Picardie" sur la commune de Gurgy (Yonne)', *Rev. arch. de l'Est et du Centre-Est*, xxxi, 7–54.

Piggott, S. 1950. 'Swords and scabbards of the British Early Iron Age', *P.P.S.* xvi, 1–28.

Polenz, H. 1977. 'Ein Eimer vom Aylesford-Typus aus Geisenheim im Rheingau', *Nassauische Annalen*, lxxxviii, 9–34.

Rieth, A. 1969. 'Zur Herstellungstechnik der Eisendolche der späten Hallstattzeit', *Jahrb. R.G.Z. Mainz*, xvi, 17–58.

Schüle, W. 1969. *Die Meseta-Kulturen der iberischen Halbinsel*, Berlin.

Sherlock, R. L. 1962. *London and Thames Valley*, British Regional Geology, 3rd edn.

Smith, R. A. 1905. *A Guide to the Antiquities of the Early Iron Age*, British Museum.

—— 1908. 'The Weybridge bucket, and prehistoric trade with Italy', *Surrey Arch. Coll.* xxi, 165–9.

—— 1918. 'Specimens from the Layton Collection, in Brentford Public Library', *Archaeologia*, lxix, 1–30.

—— 1925. *A Guide to the Antiquities of the Early Iron Age*, British Museum, 2nd edn.

Spratling, M. G. 1970. 'The smiths of South Cadbury', *Current Arch.* xviii, 188–91.

—— 1972. 'Southern British decorated bronzes of the Late Pre-Roman Iron Age', unpublished Ph.D. thesis, London University.

—— 1979. 'The debris of metal working', in G. J. Wainwright, *Gussage All Saints: an Iron Age settlement in Dorset*, London.

Stead, I. M. 1965. 'The Celtic chariot', *Antiquity*, xxix, 259–65.

—— 1971. 'The reconstruction of Iron Age buckets from Aylesford and Baldock', in G. de G. Sieveking (ed.), *Prehistoric and Roman Studies* (= *B. M. Quarterly*, xxxv, 250–82).

—— 1976. 'The earliest burials of the Aylesford Culture', in G. de G. Sieveking *et al.* (eds.), *Problems in Economic and Social Archaeology*, London, 401–16.

—— 1979. *The Arras Culture*, York.

—— 1983. 'La Tène swords and scabbards in Champagne', *Germania*, lxi, 487–511.

Stjernquist, B. 1967. *Ciste a Cordoni (Rippenzisten)*, Acta Arch. Lundensia, ser. 4, no. vi.

Strong, D. E. 1967. 'Silver cup', in I. M. Stead, 'A La Tène III burial at Welwyn Garden City', *Archaeologia*, ci, 1–62.

Szabó, M. 1974. Review of de Navarro 1972, in *Acta Arch. Acad. Scient. Hung.* xxvi, 246–51.

Thill, G. 1967. 'Die Metallgegenstände aus vier spätlatènezeitlichen Brandgräbern bei Goeblingen-Nospelt', *Hémecht*, xix, 87–98.

Vidal, M. 1976. 'Le seau de bois orné de Vieille-Toulouse (Haute-Garonne)', *Gallia*, xxxiv, 167–200.

Vulliamy, C. E. 1930. *The Archaeology of Middlesex and London*, London.

Wamser, G. 1975. 'Zur Hallstattkultur in Ostfrankreich. Die Fundgruppen im Jura und in Burgund', *Ber. R.G.K.* lvi, 1–178.

Wardman, A. M. 1972. 'The Early La Tène brooches of the British Isles', unpublished B.A. thesis, The Queen's University, Belfast.

Werner, J. 1955. 'Die Nauheimer Fibel', *Jahrb. R.G.Z. Mainz*, ii, 170–95.

—— 1978. 'Zur Bronzekanne von Kelheim', *Bayer. Vorgeschichtsbl.* xliii, 1–18.

Wolseley, G., Smith, R. A. and Hawley, W. 1927. 'Prehistoric and Roman settlements on Park Brow', *Archaeologia*, lxxvi, 1–40.

Wood-Martin, W. G. 1886. *The Lake Dwellings of Ireland*, Dublin.

Wyss, R. 1968. 'Belege zur keltischen Schwertschmiedekunst', in E. Schmid *et al.* (eds.), *Provincialia: Festschrift für Rudolf Laur-Belart*, Basel/Stuttgart.

Alet and Cross-Channel Trade

Loïc Langouët

This study is concerned primarily with results obtained from discoveries on the site of Alet and with their interpretation in the context of the period. I will also try to consider the relationship between Alet and Britain, and more particularly between Alet and Hengistbury Head.

Alet

Alet, in Saint-Malo, is a 14-ha. peninsula situated to the east of the river Rance, near its mouth, and accessible from the mainland by a narrow, sandy isthmus. Since 1973 the Centre Régional Archéologique d'Alet has organized five annual seasons of excavation in the central urban zone of this promontory. During each season, an archaeological layer containing dense pre-Roman occupation was studied. Moreover, during various municipal works, the same occupation layer was identified in other areas of Alet (fig. 21). The remains found within this clay layer, covering the granitic sand and the bed-rock, allow us to reconstruct the main features of the pre-Roman occupation.

The structures

Alet was also a Gallo-Roman and medieval town which was deserted in the mid-twelfth century in favour of the island of Saint-Malo (Langouët 1976). During recent excavations various pre-Roman features were recognized among later walls, pits and ditches. These features are essentially post-holes, ditches, grain-storage pits, and domestic and industrial hearths. It was, however, difficult to establish the relationship between the different features in order to reconstruct the main outlines of the pre-Roman settlement, because of the incompleteness and discontinuity of what was recovered.

Grain-storage pits dug out of the rock had an average diameter of 80 cm. and an average depth of 60 cm., and querns were discovered in the pre-Roman occupation

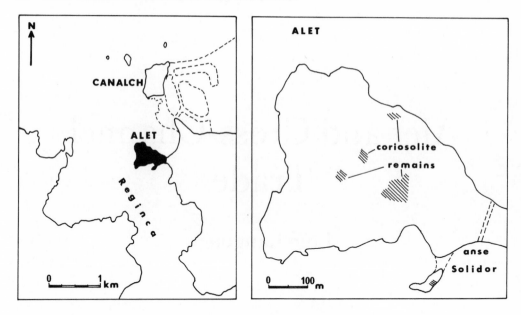

FIG. 21. The settlement at Alet: Location map

layer. An interesting metallurgical installation was also found: it was used to produce a copper-silver alloy, copper and silver having been extracted from ores of argentiferous lead and copper (Maréchal 1979). In a formless, burnt clay structure many objects, in the form of heavy cupellation dishes with average diameters of 10 cm., constituted the residues of metal-working. These residues contain an average of 40 per cent lead, 20 per cent copper and 4 per cent silver. The silver composition is found near the upper surface of these residues, which indicate the preparation of a copper-silver alloy. Crucibles of the same form but with a different composition were found at Hengistbury Head (Bushe-Fox 1915, 78). Perhaps these discoveries at Alet are related to the minting of Coriosolitan coins, as the relative proportions of copper (55–70 per cent) and of silver (25 per cent) in the coins (Gruel 1981) are consistent with the chemical analyses of the residues.

It is mainly objects found in the upper part of the mica-rich clay layer which provide information about pre-Roman occupation at Alet, in the absence of clear structures. As the majority of the finds are of local origin they provide interesting evidence for the indigenous way of life, but the small quantity of imported objects is sufficient also to define economic contacts and the precise chronology of the site.

Material from the settlement at Alet

Pre-Roman material was discovered both within the archaeological layer, and among the displaced rubbish of later times which resulted from Gallo-Roman and medieval building activity from the first to the tenth centuries A.D. The material basically comprises:

Very numerous (over 3,000) sherds of local wares (Langouët 1978a)

Imported wares, generally fine or decorated pottery (Langouët 1978a)
Fragments of Dressel 1A and Pascual 1 amphorae (Sanquer 1978)
Numerous animal bones (Poulain 1979)
Very numerous limpet shells (up to 3 kg. per square metre)
Gaulish coins, mainly Coriosolitan (Langouët 1978b)
Many iron objects and iron slag
Spindle-whorls and stone pestles
Jewellery (brooches, rings and pendants) (Galliou 1975)
Pieces of salt moulds imported from the bay of Mont Saint-Michel
Various other objects

These objects provide evidence for the nature of domestic life, and for a variety of activities.The importance of the local metallurgical industry is shown by the presence of slag residues and tools. These discoveries are important because we do not have any similar material from the north coast of Armorica, from Saint Brieuc to Avranches. Let us attempt to analyse the evidence provided by these discoveries.

The pottery from Alet (fig. 22)

A minimum of 401 local vessels were identified, based on the study of rims and bases (Langouët 1978a). The bases were generally flat (98 per cent), and the micaceous pastes mainly black (35 per cent) or grey (47 per cent). Sixteen forms

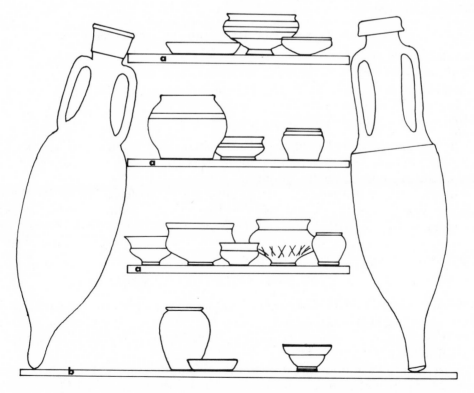

FIG. 22. Local (a) and imported (b) pottery found at Alet. Scale *c.* 1:12

were differentiated, the most common being a necked bowl which has a cordon, groove or step at the base of the neck. The average diameter of the rims of these bowls is 140 mm. The bodies are often decorated with a variety of burnished patterns (vertical and horizontal lines and hachuring). Many vessels are graphite-coated on the neck or body and, statistically, the grey vessels are rougher than the black. Seven examples of a very fine black ware (designated NF) were also found: the paste is poor in mica and relatively harder. This type of vessel was recognized at Le Petit Celland, near Avranches (Wheeler and Richardson 1957), and at Hengistbury Head (Cunliffe 1978, 46). Its surface is very highly burnished and its body decorated with groups of raised cordons, which seem to be a diagnostic typological feature.

At Hengistbury Head this fine black ware carries a cordon at the 'waist', as also do several other imported vessels of the class 1 defined by Barry Cunliffe. But at Alet and at Le Petit Celland this cordon is virtually absent: of the 125 bowls found in the excavations at Alet only one has a cordon at the 'waist' (Langouët 1978a), and the same small proportion applies at Le Petit Celland—approximately 2 per cent. It is probable that at Hengistbury Head, in class 1, there are also vessels which came from the territory of the Coriosolites and from other regions, especially Normandy or the Cotentin. Among the vessels analysed by Ian Freestone and Valery Rigby, whose study was kindly sent to me, there were wares similar to some from Alet (cordoned wares and rilled wares).

The coins from Alet

In the pre-Roman layer twenty-six Armorican coins were discovered:

Coriosolites—21
Turones—2
Abrincates—1
Leuci—1 (Gard region)
Veliocasses—1 (homotype) (Langouët 1978b)

To the first group can be added seven Coriosolitan coins found out of context. The collection contains 85 per cent of Coriosolitan coins, reflecting the importance of Alet in the economy of the Coriosolites.

J.-B. Colbert de Beaulieu (1973) established a chronological order for the six classes of Coriosolitan issues, and used the idea of 'facies' (composition by classes as percentages of the whole). Lately, on the basis of chemical analyses of alloys and the relationships between die-types, Katherine Gruel redefined this chronological order, from earliest to latest, as follows:

VI   V   IV   I   III   II   (Gruel 1981)

Between classes V and IV Katherine Gruel found a 25 per cent reduction in the silver content, and between classes IV and I a change in the dies of the reverses. Both these changes she associates with events in Armorica related to the conquest of Gaul, in 56 B.C.

Apart from isolated finds, great quantities of Coriosolitan coins have been found in hoards in Armorica and in Jersey (Colbert de Beaulieu 1973). On the basis of composition by issue we can compare groups of different hoards from Jersey

TABLE 1

Coin groups at Alet and elsewhere compared on the basis of percentage composition by issue

Class	VI	V	IV	I	III	II
Petit Celland (20)	0	0	0	15	20	65
Jersey-6 (125)	0.8	9.6	8	15.2	13.6	52.8
Jersey-9 (9254)	0.2	3.3	5.3	14.4	22.5	54.4
Jersey-5 (740)	0.2	9.2	5.5	15.1	14.5	55.3
Jersey-11 (540)	0.2	2.1	2.8	12.3	16.8	65.6
Jersey-2 (26)	7.4	14.8	3.7	3.7	25.9	44.4
Jersey (mean values)	1.8	7.8	5.1	12.1	18.7	54.5
Alet (pre-Roman layer) (21)	0	15	0	10	30	45
Alet (total) (28)	0	17.8	0	7.1	28.5	46
Britain (25)	8		18.5		4	26	44

The facies of Alet and Britain are very similar except for the oldest class (VI). The facies of Britain and Jersey-2 are the same.

with the collection from Le Petit Celland (table 1), and we see a great similarity between their compositions. The battle between Armorican forces led by Viridorix and the Roman troops led by Sabinus is thought to have been fought at Le Petit Celland in 56 B.C.; after their defeat, described by Caesar, some of the scattered Coriosolites probably made their way across the Cotentin and passed over to Jersey with their treasure, which would account for this similarity.

The coin assemblage from Alet, characterized by high proportions of classes I, III, and II, is also comparable to the small Petit Celland collection. The Alet coin group therefore shows a typical composition for the period of the end of independence. In the pre-Roman layer excavated at Alet a Republican Roman coin was found (Langouët 1978b): a worn bronze as, minted at Lyon between 10 B.C. and A.D. 21, with a reverse showing the altar of Roma and Augustus. It is clear from the dating evidence provided by this discovery that the composition of the Coriosolitan coin assemblage remained constant after the end of independence, possibly until 10 B.C., and more probably until Romanization was effected. It is more than probable that in the intermediate period between the conquest and Romanization, from about 20 B.C., a prohibition on minting was enforced, thus stabilizing the facies of the Coriosolitan coins.

Because later coins were included in some hoards from Jersey (Le Catillon and Rozel), it is apparent that these were buried a long time after the conquest (Colbert de Beaulieu 1957); their compositions show similarities with Alet, but for different reasons, principally insular isolation.

Other imported materials, which will now be detailed, allow us to define the chronological limits of occupation at Alet.

Imported material at Alet

Imported objects were found throughout the pre-Roman layer, but it must be stressed that only a small percentage of the total number of finds was involved—for instance only fifteen imported pottery vessels were recovered as opposed to 401 local ones. The imports comprised the following:

A variety of brooches, one example similar to Almgren type 16, for which Patrick Galliou has suggested a date in the first century A.D. (Galliou 1975).

Several sherds of a comb-decorated ware; an import from central Gaul of *c.* A.D. 0–40 (Langouët 1978a, 65).

A Drag. 27 from southern Gaul; an early product, but certainly later than A.D. 15.

A cylinder beaker decorated with 'palmettes'. It is one of the thin-walled beakers which are generally found in early first-century contexts, especially of Augustan or Tiberian date (Galliou 1981).

Pompeian Red ware, difficult to date but produced during the first century A.D. (Peacock 1977). Dr. Peacock has examined our sherds and thinks that the pottery found at Alet belongs to his fabric 6, for which he suggests an origin in Flanders.

Numerous sherds in micaceous wares, with several grooves on the rims (a minimum of eleven vessels). This type was produced in the area between the Loire and the Seine, probably near Orléans, in the period from Caesar to Claudius (Ferdière 1972). There are sherds of this type in south-east Britain (Odiot, forthcoming).

In addition to fifteen Dressel 1A or 1B amphorae, a Pascual 1 amphora (Sanquer 1978). This last type was produced from the Augustan period onwards, but in Armorica it seems more common between A.D. 10 and 50.

On the basis of these imported objects, it seems certain that the settlement at Alet was deserted by *c.* A.D. 15–20. Moreover, the excavations have shown that the abandonment was violent and sudden. Patrick Galliou has suggested that it was a result of local disorders associated with the Gaulish uprisings in the Tiberian period described by Tacitus (Galliou 1980). In any case we must see in this abandonment the effect of a political decision. The date limit A.D. 15–20 theoretically defines the end of Coriosolitan coin production, but it is clear that the coins ceased to circulate before this date limit in Gaul. On the other hand the founding of the settlement at Alet must be placed before the conquest of Gaul, probably *c.* 80 B.C.

The main direction of import of some materials is from the south-east (micaceous wares, thin-walled beakers, comb-decorated pottery, Turonic coins, samian ware). So it is clear that after the conquest Alet had some connection with central Gaul, although it seems to have been a weak one. That there was some coastal trade seems to be illustrated by the presence of Dressel 1A and 1B and Pascual 1 amphorae, and of Pompeian Red ware.

It is important to note that the inhabitants of Alet continued to live in the traditional Gaulish style for some sixty years after the conquest. The occupation was continuous, with no break in the archaeological layer.

The analysis of the animal bones completes our information. Of 3,000 bones found during the excavation of living sites and rubbish pits, *c.* 2,500 were identified, representing a minimum number of 133 animals (Poulain 1979). The domestic animals constituted 86 per cent of the fauna. Stock-raising was based mainly on sheep (32 per cent), pigs (26 per cent) and cattle (19 per cent), adults representing 83 per cent of the animal population. Limpet shells were found in very dense concentrations (3 kg. per square metre in some areas), but there were no oyster or mussel shells.

Alet and cross-Channel trade

The relative isolation of Alet after the Romanization of Gaul is, however, compensated by its relationship with southern Britain, which is evidenced mainly by coins and pottery.

The Coriosolitan coinage found in Britain establishes the main period of contact between Alet and Britain. The composition of the British coin assemblage has been calculated (table 1: classes IV and V are combined) from the classes of imported Coriosolitan coins defined by D. F. Allen (1961). The table shows that classes I, II and III are very well represented, making up the majority of coins. Thus most of the Coriosolitan coins in Britain appear to have been exported either during or after the conquest of Gaul (in Armorica, 56 B.C.). Earlier contacts are, however, indicated by the class VI coins and by Dressel 1A amphorae; but in the last interim report (1981) on the excavations at Hengistbury Head, kindly sent to me by Barry Cunliffe, this late date would seem to be corroborated, since Gaulish imports appear to occur slightly later in the sequence, after the imports of Dressel 1A amphorae. On the southern coast, Hengistbury seems to be the centre of diffusion of Armorican coins, and Coriosolitan coins clearly constitute the majority of imported coins.

Hengistbury Head is in Durotrigian territory, and perhaps we can see evidence for a reverse flow of trade in the presence of Durotrigian coins in the Le Catillon hoard in Jersey. This contact between the Coriosolites and the Durotriges is also evidenced by the appearance in the latter's territory of Armorican pottery containing mica or 'amphiboles'. However, the precise origins of the pottery found at Hengistbury are still not known and should be sought in Brittany and Normandy, perhaps especially in the Cotentin. We can perhaps see evidence of contact with Normandy in the presence of ovoid multi-cordoned wares at Hengistbury. This type of ware is found mainly in the Eure (Alizay, Lery and Caudebec-lès-Elboeuf), but also in the Mayenne (Moulay), in Guernsey (Catioroc) and in Finistère (Plouegat-Moysan).

The Peutinger Table would appear to give us vital information about cross-Channel trade in the pre-Roman period, and in it we can identify the Condate–Fanum, Martis–Reginca and Rennes–Corseul–Alet roads (Langouët 1980). This evidence can be coupled with results from excavations in Alet's Roman harbour and the investigation of a pump for distributing water to shipping (Langouët and Meury 1976; Langouët 1978c). After the abandonment of Alet in *c.* A.D. 15–20, a port survived at the foot of the promontory of Alet, whose main pumping system was dated to the first or second century A.D. The port's name, Reginca in the Peutinger Table, remains with us today in the name of the river Rance (Langouët 1980). Another name, I. Lenur, appears in the Peutinger Table in the middle of the Channel (Quentel 1976), and this must be a reference to the Channel Islands. Thus we have evidence for the Alet–Channel Islands route in the Peutinger Table, a route also indicated by the distribution of pre-Roman pottery. The names recorded in the Table are pre-Roman (Lenur and Reginca); the retention of these two names argues against a Roman or Gallo-Roman foundation and in favour of their existence prior to the Gallo-Roman period. Furthermore, a pre-Roman stage in the Gallo-Roman water-supply system of Reginca (Anse Solidor in Saint-Malo) has been identified, in the form of a lozenge-shaped water basin and a small channel (pl. V).

The pre-Roman lozenge-shaped water basin (bottom, centre left) in the Anse Solidor.
On this aerial view there can also be seen the Gallo-Roman rectangular water-basin
(top left) and Roman roads (right)

The present Saint-Malo–Portsmouth route by car ferry perpetuates the ancient Alet–Hengistbury Head route or, later, that of Alet–Clausentum (Fulford 1977).

Alet within the territory of the Coriosolites

To the east and west of Alet, on the coast, there are two known *oppida*: Saint-Coulomb, Le Meinga (Wheeler and Richardson 1957, 113), and Erquy, Camp-de-César (Giot *et al.* 1968 and 1969). But there are other possible *oppida* on the coast and on the banks of the river Rance (fig. 23) (Giot 1980). Our knowledge

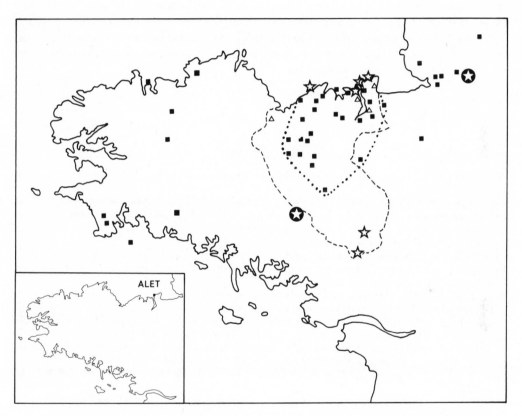

FIG. 23. The territory of the Coriosolites in the pre-Roman (.....) and Gallo-Roman (----) periods. Single coins (■); small known (☆) and possible (△) *oppida*; great *oppida* (✪).

of the rural territory of the Coriosolites is very poor: enclosures were recorded by aerial photography, but their chronology remains unknown, even after field-walking expeditions. The central territory of the Coriosolites is well defined by isolated finds of Coriosolitan coins, and in the period of Romanization we can observe an extension of the area over which these occur, which defines the Gallo-Roman *civitas* of the Coriosolites (Guennou 1981, plates).

Conclusions

Alet was an important pre-Roman settlement from *c.* 80 B.C. to A.D. 15–20. From the Augustan period on, imported material from Gaul shows that Alet's trading contacts were principally with the south-east. It seems that for Alet cross-Channel trade, especially with Hengistbury Head, was at its height between the conquest and the effective Romanization of Gaul (between *c.* 56 B.C. and 25 B.C.). During this period Alet, being immediately to the south of an independent Britain and far from Rome, was naturally greatly tempted to maintain contacts with British tribes. But taking into account the hypothesis of decreasing activity at Hengistbury Head before 25 B.C., perhaps from around 50 B.C., we must assume that trade between the Coriosolites and Hengistbury was concentrated between *c.* 56 and 50 B.C. We must suppose that a Coriosolitan navy survived after the events of 56 B.C. which involved the destruction of the Venetic navy. We must hope that future excavations at Alet, especially of the pre-Roman water installation of the Anse Solidor, will produce evidence to confirm this.

BIBLIOGRAPHY

Allen, D. F. 1961. 'The origins of coinage in Britain: a reappraisal', in S. S. Frere (ed.), *Problems of the Iron Age in Southern Britain*, London, 97–308.

Bushe-Fox, J. P. 1915. *Excavations at Hengistbury Head in 1911–1912*, Soc. Antiq. London Res. Rep. III.

Colbert de Beaulieu, J.-B. 1957. 'Le trésor de Jersey-11 et la numismatique celtique des deux Bretagnes', *Revue Belge de Numismatique*, ciii, 47–87.

—— 1973. *Traité de numismatique celtique*, Paris.

Cunliffe, B. W. 1978. *Hengistbury Head*, London.

Ferdière, A. 1972. 'Introduction à l'étude d'un type de céramique: les urnes à bord mouluré gallo-romaines précoces', *Rev. arch. de l'Est*, xxiii, 1–2.

Fulford, M. G. 1977. 'Pottery and Britain's foreign trade in the later Roman period', in D. P. S. Peacock (ed.), *Pottery and Early Commerce*, London, 35–84.

Galliou, P. 1975. 'Les objets de parure et de toilette découverts à Alet', *Dossiers du C.R.A.A.* iii, 77–86.

—— 1980. 'La première mort d'Alet: une hypothèse', *Dossiers du C.R.A.A.* viii, 37–40.

—— 1981. 'A group of early Central Gaulish beakers', in A. C. and A. S. Anderson (eds.), *Roman Pottery Research in Britain and North-West Europe*, B.A.R. IS 123, Oxford, 265–76.

Giot, P.-R. 1980. 'Aperçus sur l'âge du Fer du nord-est de la Bretagne', *Dossiers du C.R.A.A.*, C, 99–112.

Giot, P.-R., *et al.* 1968. 'Les retranchements du cap d'Erquy: les fouilles de 1967', *Ann. de Bretagne*, lxx, 67–84.

—— 1969. 'Les retranchements du cap d'Erquy: les fouilles de 1968', *Ann. de Bretagne*, lxxvi, 21–36.

Gruel, K. 1981. *Le trésor de Trébry*, Etudes de Numismatique Celtique, 1.

Guennou, G. 1981. 'La cité des Coriosolites', *Dossiers du C.R.A.A.*, D.

Langouët, L. 1976. *Alet, berceau antique de Saint Malo*, C.R.A.A.

—— 1978a. 'Les céramiques gauloises d'Alet', *Dossiers du C.R.A.A.* vi, 57–104.

—— 1978b. 'Les monnaies gauloises d'Alet', *Dossiers du C.R.A.A.* vi, 23–30.

—— 1978c. 'La site portuaire de Reginca dans la rade de Solidor à l'époque gallo-romaine', *Dossiers du C.R.A.A.*, A, 21–8.

—— 1980. 'Reginca ou Reginea', *Arch. en Bretagne*, xxvii, 7–15.

Langouët, L. and Meury, J.-P. 1976. 'Les éléments de la machinerie gallo-romaine d'Alet', *Dossiers du C.R.A.A.* iv, 113–26.

Maréchal, J. R. 1979. 'Note sur un produit metallurgique plombo-cuprifère découvert à Alet', *Dossiers du C.R.A.A.* vii, 25–30.

Peacock, D. P. S. 1977. 'Pompeian Red ware', in D. P. S. Peacock (ed.), *Pottery and Early Commerce*, London, 147–62, at pp. 157–8.

Poulain, T. 1979. 'Les vestiges de faune dans l'agglomération pré-romaine d'Alet', *Dossiers du C.R.A.A.* vii, 31–6.

Quentel, P. 1976. 'Le nom ancien des îles anglo-normandes', *Dossiers du C.R.A.A.* vi, 51–6.

Sanquer, R. 1978. 'Amphores romaines trouvées à Alet', *Dossiers du C.R.A.A.* vi, 51–6.

Wheeler, R. E. M. and Richardson, K. M. 1957. *Hill Forts of Northern France*, Soc. Antiq. London Res. Rep. xix.

Regional Groups in Western France

Alain Duval

From the Continental point of view, any attempt at the present time to define the connections between France and Britain in the protohistoric period is fraught with difficulties. Points of comparison, especially typological ones, can of course be sought in Gaul, the area closest geographically to ancient Britain. For certain classes of objects some parallels can be established, but these similarities merely prove that in a given period the same series of objects was used and the same style of decoration preferred on both sides of the Channel. To base theories of common culture or even civilization on these similarities would be to go beyond the evidence. Moreover, it should be borne in mind that each country has its own traditions of scholarship in the field of protohistoric archaeology, and it is useless for one country to try to transfer its own methods of research to a neighbouring country. Thus, the French will continue to disappoint both the British, with their formalizations, and the Germans, with their distribution maps. I do not believe that it is possible at present to know on what basis the similarities which exist between one side of the Channel and the other should be judged, which aspects would provide evidence for a common history, or the extent to which cultural areas can be defined in the pre-Roman period. And in particular I believe that where parallels can be found on the Continent for objects which occur in Britain (take, for example, the excellent work of Paul Tyers (1980) on certain types of coarse ware), some of the empty zones on the French map are merely due to gaps in our research.

I will therefore not attempt, in this short paper, to answer such vague questions but will confine myself to establishing a few basic facts, beginning with what is 'known' in French archaeology, which may perhaps help in another line of enquiry, i.e. defining once and for all the points of contact between one side of the Channel and the other. This explains my title 'Regional Groups in Western France'. I have based my approach on ideas put forward in a summary article on the Middle La Tène in the Paris Basin (Duval 1976) which is greatly in need of revision from the point of view of chronology; but for that we must await the results of work undertaken by Ian Stead and Jean-Loup Flouest (Flouest and Stead 1981) in northern Champagne as well as those of the research teams in southern Picardy (Duval and Blanchet 1976).

As a preliminary I would like to explain a number of trends in the French approach to the subject which may not always be apparent to foreign scholars. First, it is very often the same topics which are debated: What constitutes the Marnian? What was the sequence of development in funerary rites? What is an *oppidum* and what was its function? And often our scholars stay within the limits of these questions, going ever deeper into them without looking at what may be beyond. Secondly, scholars in France and in neighbouring countries are frequently limited by the present-day boundaries of regions or states: the Marnian area is described as 'l'est de la France' (Thénot 1982); Armorica as medieval or modern Brittany; Belgium has its own cultural group of La Haine (Mariën 1961). Thirdly, French publications dealing with the Iron Age are almost always concerned not with palaeoecology or economic and social issues (with a few notable exceptions, such as the work of Professor Giot) but with chronology. To provide dates as close and exact as possible is considered the mark of good scholarship, or the crowning achievement of a series of studies (Hatt and Roualet 1977). As a result, French researchers have great difficulty in dealing with subjects divorced from the main 'events' of history, i.e. what happened in the second century B.C., or at the beginning of the first century, or at the time of the Gallic Wars. The concept of long-term evolution is integrated into our studies with great difficulty.

Let us now consider the evidence that is available for an understanding of the 'archaeological geography' of the pre-Roman period. By that I am referring to areas and not boundaries, applying the protohistorical traditions which are valid for the Neolithic and the Bronze Age.

(a) *Pottery*. We need to distinguish between coarse and fine wares. They obviously do not provide the same evidence, as the first enables us to define centres of manufacture, the second areas of use. This will be shown more clearly when we come to the Marnian culture (below).

(b) *Coins*. The study of Gaulish coins (the principles of which have been excellently set out by J.-B. Colbert de Beaulieu (1973)) should be approached with caution. The basic aim is not the attribution of a particular coin to a particular 'tribe', but an understanding of the evolution of Gaulish coinage. The right to mint coins multiplied until the time of Tiberius, when it was held at the level of *pagi*. Thus in theory one can go backwards in time to larger and larger political units and, except with the earliest coinage, as far back as the time of the great empires—or, as I would prefer to call them, *mouvances* (economic areas). Unfortunately, French archaeologists do not agree with the very early dates which British numismatists suggest for the first bronze coins, nor with the very late dates suggested by French numismatists.

(c) *Luxury objects*. These are of two types. First, imports such as wine and oil amphorae from Spain or Italy, Italian pottery (Arretine and Campanian) and 'hellenistic' lamps. Secondly, objects which are considered unusual for the areas in which they are found and which could have been traded in from outside the immediate locality (i.e. an area of a few kilometres) or from outside the entire region (a few dozen up to 100 or 200 km.): these could include pottery (e.g. painted wares, or pedestal urns); certainly bronze objects (such as chariot furnishings and jewellery); gold objects (such as torcs, like those from south-west France, Hungary and Ireland); iron, either in the semi-manufactured state of currency bars or as completely finished objects such as scabbards and swords (some even with maker's marks). And these finds, just because they are unusual, indicate not only economic ties but also cultural and/or ritual ones (and that is the problem posed by the eponymous site of La Tène).

(d) *Ancient authors.* These are to be treated with critical caution, as we have already tried to demonstrate (Duval 1982), and in conjunction with the archaeological evidence. In the present context it must be stressed that the 'peoples' described by Caesar were not all at the same level in the political and social hierarchy of Gaul. For example, the Unelli of Lower Normandy were one of a number of groups scattered throughout the region, while the Ambiani of Picardy were the surviving core of an ancient empire.

(e) *The distribution and nature of settlement sites.* Where were the farms (in which areas and on what type of soil)? Where were the open settlements? How long were they occupied? How were the *oppida* distributed? (I believe them to be a centripetal phenomenon.) What was the nature of their occupation (why, for instance, were they deserted in Belgic Gaul but very densely occupied from eastern Gaul to Bohemia, sometimes spread over enormous areas and representing a major phenomenon of preurbanization)? What type of society do they represent? Were they in some cases the defended camps of the aristocracy, when they held power, and in others small fortified 'towns' of craftsmen and traders?

(f) *The cultural areas which can be defined by funerary practice.* Was pottery present or absent? Was there any metalwork and if so of what type (bronze or iron)? What type of objects were used as offerings (tools, weapons or others)? Were burials by inhumation or cremation? What was the relationship between the grave goods and the individual buried (was it an inurned burial, were weapons sacrificed, etc.)? All these aspects must of course be placed in a chronological context.

(g) *Cult centres or sanctuaries.* These indicate where the contemporary boundaries lay (see, for example, F. Dumasy's very interesting work on the Carnutes and the Senones (Dumasy 1974)) as well as the actual places of assembly and, as a corollary, help us to understand the system of communications from a geographical point of view—this is one of the most interesting questions posed by the famous site of Gournay-sur-Aronde (Brunaux and Meniel 1983). But the whole topographical question still remains to be unravelled.

Let us now briefly summarize the Marnian problem. The idea of a Marnian cultural centre corresponding, in the fifth century B.C., with an area which covers the modern French departments of Aisne, Marne and the southern Ardennes has been put forward (Duval and Blanchet 1976; Duval and Buchsenschutz 1976). The assemblage is well known (the 'Champagne culture') and easily recognized by the forms and decoration of the pottery, the types of personal ornament with distinctive combinations of shape and decoration which persisted to the end of the fourth century B.C., and, incidentally, weapons; but very few structures have been analysed. Moreover, this cultural area, which has been recognized since the nineteenth century, has provided the framework for numerous typological and chronological studies, the most recent being those by D. Bretz-Mahler (1970) and J.-J. Hatt with P. Roualet (1977) respectively.

It is generally agreed that spreading out from this centre was a vast 'Marnian' area, displaying subtle regional variations but lacking the fine pottery or the rich ornaments. This area covers the north of France, southern Champagne, Picardy, perhaps the Ile-de-France and the Orléanais. It is basically a pottery zone.

It should be possible to learn something of the social, political and economic order from this Marnian phenomenon. It is clear that there were differences within the greater Marnian area, and even its centre was not homogeneous. The western part (Aisne) is characterized by the scarcity of weapons and the lesser importance of chariot burials, and seems to be an area transitional to the more westerly regions. Therefore one cannot, as certain authors would have it, retain the concept of a vaguely defined civilization, speaking of a 'vast Marnian zone', on the basis of these slight common denominators. In my opinion, in Champagne proper there was an exceptionally important concentration of population, with many chariot (hence princely) burials, weapons and costly objects. Then, in Aisne, we have another important concentration of population, with a great deal of fine pottery from a fairly early date (as at Oulchy: Hinout and Duval, forthcoming), and still with some chariot burials, numerous ornaments, but few weapons. Beyond, the same ceramic assemblage survives, but an incomplete range. We must therefore note these three different levels (fig. 24): the Marnian (as a whole); the western Marnian

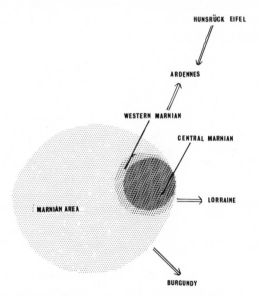

FIG. 24. Diagram showing the Marnian zone and its relationship with other cultural areas

(Picardy); the eastern Marnian (Champagne). This view is in complete agreement with that of J.-J. Hatt, who sees the simultaneous appearance of the La Tène culture *sensu stricto* in several well-defined geographical centres within continental Europe. The Marnian would be the most westerly centre, and its influence would be felt towards the west rather than the east, where other cultural centres existed.

The situation in the fourth century B.C. is complex. We see the establishment of groups different from the Marnian (the Sénonais, for example, between Burgundy, the Ile-de-France and the Orléanais), the almost complete disappearance of the western Marnian (finds are very scarce), and changes in the social hierarchy, with chariot burials becoming rare and personal ornaments more common in the Champagne area. Was this the result of overpopulation (?) owing to the great wealth of the Marnian world (?), which led to an exodus towards Italy (?) and a consequent breakdown of the existing hierarchy (?) at the same time as trade with Etruria ceased? It is now that the free style develops, and the many links within the Celtic world, and in central and eastern France the Helveto-Italic trade route becomes the dominant one—but that is outside the scope of this paper.

The Marnian disappears during the third century B.C. and at the same time the whole of Gaul seems to be assimilated into the La Tène civilization, which means that we are dealing with two contradictory phenomena. The unity of Champagne is broken. The northern part is now culturally closer to Picardy and to some extent represents the ultimate advance of western Celtic civilization. The southern part, by contrast, is closer culturally to central and eastern Gaul (especially the Sénonais).

The concept of the 'Marnian' should therefore be used in a dynamic way, and not as a mythical term for isolating classes of objects; and certainly not in the sense of a sort of ancestral area of the Gauls of the second and first centuries B.C.

I would now like to offer a few comments on Gaul in general, to place these regional groups in context.

The Celticization of the third century B.C. is accompanied by an impoverishment in grave goods—in the range of types, in quality and in the number of objects. There is a decline in the standard of bronze-working and the manufacture of fine pottery, although the decoration becomes more sophisticated. Small, organized, rural communities appear (Duval forthcoming b), each with their own local craftsmen (smiths and potters), who therefore replace the regional workshops which had predominated since the Bronze Age. A good illustration of this is the appearance of the fibula with the foot attached to the bow, of La Tène II type, which can be quickly produced from iron wire and which was therefore made by smiths who did not need a very complicated set of tools.

These developments could imply a general impoverishment of the population, with a way of life now based on small, self-sufficient rural communities typical of non-urbanized countries. But at the same time one might see them as marking a transition to a truly agricultural economy, thanks to the now fully mastered iron technology, with a kind of second revolution after the Neolithic implied by the appearance of a wide range of tools, which are regarded as valuable items since they are frequently deposited with burials (knives/shears/'razors', and later axes). We must not therefore (especially in north-western Gaul) dismiss the hypothesis of clearances and the bringing into cultivation of heavy soils, such as those of Picardy. The unity of the Celtic world of the second and first centuries B.C. would thus be an economic one and we should recognize, in addition to Mediterranean Europe and Germanic Europe, a middle Europe made rich through her agricultural economy and arousing the envy of her neighbours (52 B.C.—Alesia; 9 B.C.—the destruction of the Boii by the Marcomanni).

It is clear that the way of life changed. We have no direct evidence to show this, but must turn to later sources. Caesar speaks of *aedificia:* we do not know whether this means native farms or forerunners of the *villa*. However, the latter cannot have appeared out of nothing, and one would expect to see continuity at least in their economic role. In my opinion the great building at Verberie (Oise) (Blanchet and Buchsenschutz 1983), datable to the end of the second century B.C., was such a forerunner and belonged to a major landowner.

The Picardian model, of a region dotted with large farms, cannot however be extended throughout the whole of Gaul. Nor are aerial photographs of these establishments (now known to be numerous) sufficient in themselves—more excavations will need to be carried out. In the present state of knowledge we can only put forward the question: are forerunners of the Gallo-Roman *villa* only to be found in Belgic Gaul, for economic and social reasons (heavier soils and a more powerful landed aristocracy, as shown by the hill-forts), or do they occur throughout Gaul?

To sum up, it seems reasonable to suggest that Gaul at the end of the Middle La Tène and in the Final La Tène was basically agricultural, with a population mainly involved in a subsistence economy, albeit a very hierarchical one in which great landowners held the power. Indeed, it is curious to see aristocratic tombs reappearing in western Gaul, provided with weapons and luxury items (e.g. those at Châtillon-sur-Indre in Berry). One particular group of chariot burials stands out, basically centred on Belgic Gaul between Hannogne (Ardennes) and Inglemare (Seine-Maritime) (Duval 1975a and b). I have counted twelve—a considerable number—with two outliers at Tesson in Saintonge and Boé on the borders of Aquitaine, in the territory of the Nitiobriges of the Agenais. The grave goods reveal a trade in luxury items (one can see parallels between pieces from Paris, La Courte in Belgium and Mezek in Bulgaria). This trade begins at the start of the third century B.C. and involves gold and bronze jewellery (including 'pseudofiligree' work: Duval 1977), vessels and, of course, weapons. There seem to have been two main trade routes: first of all via the Danube, from Pannonia and the territory of the Scordisci, and later from Italy via the Narbonnaise. This explains the important role of the Saône valley, situated at the crossing point of these two routes.

The landed aristocracy seems to have depended on a warrior class, clearly recognizable in the cemeteries by their heavy iron weapons, consisting of shields with bosses and edge bindings, spears with butts, and large swords hung from the belt by a suspension-loop of twisted chain. Their ornaments, when they have them, are enormous iron fibulae, as at Saint-Maur or Epiais-Rhus in the Paris region (Lardy 1983). To begin with, these warriors were buried by inhumation, but gradually the rite changed to cremation, with weapons as sacrificial offerings. Similar weapons occur in the 'great sanctuaries', but there the funerary aspect still remains to be studied and we must await the definitive work of Jean-Louis Brunaux which is shortly to be published.

It must have been the trade generated by an aristocracy in control of great wealth which led to the appearance of the first gold coins in Gaul, but these did not, in the third century B.C., constitute a true monetary economy. In the areas peripheral to Celtic Gaul, objects might have been made 'to order' for non-Celtic or only recently Celticized princes. (We are obliged to refer to 'peripheral areas' when speaking of regions like Normandy or Saintonge at these early dates in the absence of much in the way of finds, especially pottery.) That is why the Amfreville (Eure) and Agris (Charente) helmets have been interpreted as products of this sort, non-functional and displaying a range of stylistic affinities derived from a variety of sources, as is the case with some objects from Ireland (Duval and Schaaf, and Gomez, in progress).

Against this background we must ask what was happening at the regional level from the end of the third century B.C., after the decline of the Marnian. I have studied this question with respect to the Paris Basin, on the basis of funerary rites and deposits in cemeteries, and the conclusions of this study are not in dispute. Without going into too much detail, it is clear that there are two completely contrasting regions:

(i) *The Sénonais.* Here the burial rite was inhumation for a long time. Iron objects, especially weapons, were often deposited, but there were few bronze objects and pottery was very rare. Cremation appeared late, and weapons were ritually deposited in warrior burials.

(ii) *Picardy.* The situation here was exactly the opposite. Cremation appeared early, from the end of the third century B.C. Metalwork was rare, with few iron and almost no bronze objects, but among the iron objects brooches and personal articles ('razors'/shears/knives) predominate. There are no weapons (are they to be found in the sanctuaries?). On the other hand pottery is plentiful. This is the situation in the main cemetery at Breuil-le-Sec (Degenne and Duval 1983), where out of twelve burials excavated, nine contained more than four kinds of pottery and sometimes there was a wide range of types including several bowl forms, both tall and short, a significant proportion of which were decorated.

The other regions group themselves between these two extremes: Upper Normandy, fairly late on, in the first century B.C., and northern Champagne are, with some subtle differences, closer to the Picardy model; southern Champagne and perhaps Burgundy are closer to that of the Sénonais. It is around Picardy that we find the first evidence of the Belgae, characterized at the funerary level by the features just described, much more than by the pedestal urn which appears frequently only because pottery is so abundant in burials. These Belgae are also characterized by a more marked aristocratic structure than elsewhere, with large farms and chariot burials. It leads us to wonder whether the similarities between one side of the Channel and the other were not socio-economic *before* being cultural and, *a fortiori*, ethnic.

New features appear at the end of the second and beginning of the first centuries B.C. They are well known in France and, in the light of recent archaeological research, certain facts are fairly widely accepted. We see a well-structured society headed by a landed aristocracy which becomes progressively more decadent. Most of our knowledge is related to political history: some of the powerful 'tribes' still exist (the Ambiani, Veneti, Pictones, etc.); the aristocracy still owns the land; princes of royal blood are identified by names ending in *-rix* (Ambiorix, Vercingetorix); this aristocracy is far from defunct, as princely burials, including chariot burials, show; this is the great epoch of anthropoid daggers (Clarke and Hawkes 1955). Warrior burials occur throughout Gaul, and so still do beautiful gold objects, such as the torc from Mailly-le-Camp bearing an inscription naming the Nitiobroges (or Nitiobriges) of the Agenais.

But new tendencies become apparent. Caesar gives us a very curious picture of Gaul in the process of crumbling, with some areas, like Upper Normandy, completely fragmented; others, such as Armorica, fairly divided; and still others retaining a strong unity, as in central Gaul around the territory of the Arverni. What is clear is that there is a general tendency for large units to be split into *pagi*, but that the process is not the same in every region.

Undoubtedly these territorial transformations are linked to changes in the political and administrative order. The right to strike coins is still spreading, perhaps indicating a succession of *de facto* declarations of independence. The first coins copied are the staters of Philip of Macedon, then coins with a rose on the reverse from Rosas (Rhode) and Agrigentum, and Tarentine half-staters, then the Syracusan tetradrachm, and finally the Massiliote potin coin and the Roman denarius. The process occurred in the context of complex developments, which would take too long to explain here, within the various zones (in the sense in which J.-B. Colbert de Beaulieu refers to the 'denarius zone') (fig. 25). The vicissitudes of the Armorican stater, fluctuating between gold, silver and bronze, the copies of Roman denarii, and especially the first potin coins, would have been used in exchanges of a very different kind to those for which the more modest coins of previous periods were used, being part of a true exchange economy.

We must now reconsider the *De Bello Gallico* with all this is mind (Duval forthcoming b): there we see a contrast between a landed aristocracy, supporting the Gaul of the Empires, and a 'bourgeoisie', supporting a Gaul open to trade with Marseilles and Rome, not content with a purely agricultural and self-contained economy. This contrast is manifested by tensions within single populations, by political divisions, clan quarrels, quarrels even within one family, and the appearance of independent groups, the best example of which seems to be the Parisii on the borders of Belgic Gaul, east-central Gaul and Armorica who, archaeologically speaking, were not a distinct unit.

It is within this context that the appearance of hill-forts and *oppida* must be seen, a question which I do not intend to discuss here. However, the problem is not one of defining their function by typological criteria (here we differ from the German school with their questions of what is preurban and what is not, what is a 'true' *oppidum* and what is merely a hill-fort, etc.) but of considering the phenomenon in its entirety and attributing reasons for it. This approach is all too often obscured in France, where the trend is towards trying to define each hill-top site, as soon as it is recognized, as the 'capital' of a people—which is nonsense, archaeologically speaking. Reasons of defence, though important, are not the main consideration; the reasons for occupying such a site are basically economic and political. Accessibility is essential, and a location on a trade route—hence the increase in the use of these sites after the Roman conquest. (Obviously in a rural, self-sufficient society with little need for trade other solutions must be found.) The first settlements were 'open' sites (e.g. Variscourt in Picardy, Basle in Switzerland, Aulnat in Auvergne, Levroux in Berry), where we find Dressel 1A amphorae, the first potin coins, glass, bronze objects (not very many), jewellery, iron tools and some painted pottery. Then, but fairly late in many cases, we encounter hill-top sites which have the advantage over their predecessors of being more defensible, capable of being more strongly fortified (as in the case of promontory forts), of being visible from a distance and finally of being situated on uncultivated land

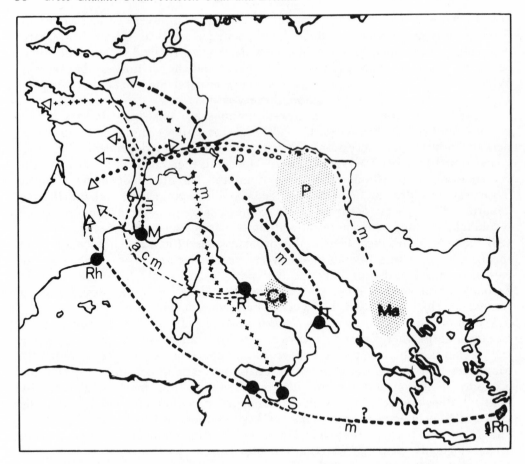

FIG. 25. Evidence of contacts between Gaul and other regions in the third to first centuries B.C.: Rhodes (Rh) to Languedoc via Agrigentum (A) and Rosas (Rhode) (Rh)—coins with rose on reverse; from Syracuse (S) to Armorica—tetradrachm; from Tarentum (T) to Belgic Gaul—half-stater; from Rome (R) to the whole of Gaul— denarii, amphorae, pottery from Campania (Ca); from Marseilles (M) to central and east-central Gaul—obols and potin coins; from Macedonia (Ma) to Arvernian Gaul—'Philippics'; from Pannonia (P) to central Gaul—gold ornaments
a = amphorae; c = pottery; m = coins; p = ornaments
The dotted lines are purely hypothetical and in no way indicate the actual routes followed

originally used as pasture. The activities within these hill-forts were the same as in the open settlements but at a more sophisticated level, with separate craftsmen's quarters, more imported items and the reappearance of bronzework. I have suggested that the inhabitants of these hill-top sites represent a new social class, opposed to the landed aristocracy, although there were a number of exceptions. And the question which follows from this should be considered: was there in fact a dual power structure in some areas of Gaul, on the one hand organized around the great landed estates, on the other around the hill-forts?

Let us now try to formalize the various factors outlined above, while

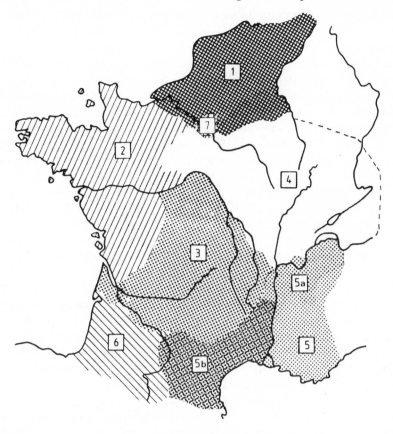

FIG. 26. The cultural regions of Gaul. 1. Belgic Gaul; 2. Armorican Gaul; 3. Central Gaul; 4. Eastern Gaul; 5. Narbonnaise, the Roman Provincia (a, Celtic; b, non-Celtic); 6. Aquitaine; 7. The territory of the Parisii

attempting to understand the regional differences. Of course, since all these processes were dynamic rather than static it is difficult to know which were exactly contemporary, and herein lie the constraints on our hypotheses. We will start with a map of Gaul as a whole which has already been put forward (fig. 26). (I have already referred to the question of the Parisii.) The basic idea which underlies this map is that we can distinguish a western and an eastern Gaul, the latter extending as far as Bohemia, showing that we must not be misled by frontiers which belonged to Roman Gaul.

Belgic Gaul. This was clearly defined by Caesar. Its southern boundary was the Risle, then the Seine. Its eastern boundary is unclear, the Remi seeming to be autonomous, although in terms of funerary practice they were related to the rest of Belgic Gaul. This region used an early system of coinage based on the Tarentine half-stater, undoubtedly centred on the Ambiani, who exercised a hegemony over the area until a very late date. Belgic Gaul is characterized by native farms; cremation burials with abundant pottery, including pedestal urns (but the decorative motifs and their techniques are more significant); chariot burials; a dominant aristocracy (cf. Caesar's passages on the Bellovaci and the Nervii); the initial coinage is succeeded by the potin coin, which becomes the current coinage of the south-east of this region for exchange purposes (and which I believe derived from the potin coins of Marseilles); and occupation in *oppida* similar to those of the more northerly regions, although the further north one goes the more the hill-forts appear to have had a purely defensive role, without permanent occupation.

Aquitaine. This is a difficult area to define, but we must try to end the confusion arising on the one hand from maps which include Aquitaine as part of Celtica (*Gallia togata*) and on the other from the archaeological reality demonstrated by G. Fabre (1952) and J.-P. Mohen (1979), who make it clear that Celtic finds in Aquitaine remain the exception, at least until the first century B.C. We have instead a completely distinct culture, which Fabre was wrong to label 'Hallstattien prolongé', but which is not Celtic either. The confusion derives from two areas belonging to a region known vaguely as the 'south-west' by the modern traveller: the first comprises Périgord and Quercy, the territories of the Petrocorii and the Cadurci, which are in fact provinces of the Massif Central, and belong culturally to the Arvernian and Languedocian region which we will deal with presently. The second comprises Bordelais and Agenais in the northern part, which are truly Celtic. Finds are common in areas which also have Celtic names: the Tayac treasure, the great settlement of Lacoste in the territory of the Bituriges Vivisci (Vivisci = Basque), the Agen helmet, the chariot burial at Boé in the territory of the Nitiobriges (whose name appears on the torc from Mailly-le-Camp in southern Champagne). Between these two tribes is the non-Celtic territory of the Ausci, a name which seems to be derived from Vasci. The pottery in these Celtic areas appears to be much influenced by that of Languedoc.

From this point on we are dealing with the third Gaul, which was called *togata*. One result of archaeological research undertaken in Gaul has been to show that this *Gallia togata* has no political or economic reality, and that there is no archaeological evidence for it before the Roman conquest. As a result (and in this I follow Daphne Nash) there is no evidence for the existence of a vast Arvernian empire.

Armorica is the third region which we must accept. Colleagues better qualified than myself have studied the sites and cultural complexes, and I take my stand on a purely geographical definition of an area between Belgic Gaul and Aquitaine, or between the Risle and the Garonne. The distinctiveness of pottery types, techniques and decoration is evident from the beginning of the third century and poses problems of this area's relationship with eastern Gaul (Giot 1971), just as, later on, the coinage of the Aulerci Cenomani seems to be similar to that of the Treveri. There seems to have been an early coinage in Armorica, perhaps controlled by the Veneti, which I believe was based on the Syracusan tetradrachm and influenced by the Macedonian stater, and this would explain the fluctuations between the use of gold and silver. But this vast zone is also part of a trade route, where archaic and archaizing objects have been found whose significance has not been investigated up to now. A spectacular example is that of the helmets found at Amfreville (in Belgic Gaul but not far distant), Tronoën (Brittany) and, a recent discovery by J. Gomez, at Agris (Saintonge). Despite certain variations which are difficult to define because of the relative scarcity of finds, the area shows some homogeneity in certain types of pottery and coins (the coinage of the Pictones is related to the coinages of Brittany, as also is the coinage of the Baiocassi of Lower Normandy).

According to this hypothesis we have an Atlantic Gaul, with sub-divisions, contrasted with a continental Gaul. Is this so surprising, or in any way different from what we know of the prehistory of France from the Bronze Age on? And on an economic and commercial level, in addition to the traditional great east–west trade routes we must consider the possible trade routes within western Gaul, and hence the role as a crossroads played by areas like the Bordelais, the 'seuil du Poitou', Berry and the entire Paris region.

Continental Gaul falls beyond the scope of this short study, but the central region poses a problem. There was certainly an economic area controlled by the Arverni, and it is for this region, between the Loire, the Rhône and the Garonne, that we must reserve the term 'Arvernian Empire'. According to some sources we should include Languedoc (*Volci Arecomici et Tectosagi*), but there seems to be a complete split between regions using gold coinage and those using silver: in central Gaul *sensu stricto* the Macedonian staters appear, but in Languedoc we find the silver coins with a rose on the reverse (often called Rhodian, but indubitably from Agrigentum and from Rosas (Rhode) in Catalunya). In Languedoc wheel-turned and combed pottery predominated from a fairly early period, while the pottery of the central area was closer typologically to that of eastern Gaul, but with its own distinctive forms and decoration (Aulnat-type bowls, and painted pottery of a different style to that of southern Germany, Dauphiné and Switzerland). Most of the rich jewellery of the third and second centuries B.C. is found on sites at the border of these two regions (Montans, Fenouillet, Lasgraïsses, Aurillac).

There remains *Eastern Gaul* which, from the third century B.C., was completely separate: contacts with Switzerland and Italy are apparent in Burgundy and southern Champagne, warrior burials with heavy iron weapons occurred very early on, distinctive objects, such as torcs with triple motifs, appear and there is no early coinage. Developments in the second and first centuries B.C. (which would take too long to elaborate here) show a division into two areas: on the one hand we have a vast central-European zone extending approximately from Berry to Bohemia, a territory graced by 'true' *oppida* in which the finds show great consistency, as J. Déchelette pointed out; on the other we have a zone very open to Romanizing influences, especially in the western part where we find potin coins copying the bronze coins of Marseilles (La Tour 5253, 5368 and 5393) and silver denarii copying those of Sulla, and an increasingly abundant trade in Campanian ware, Italian sigillata and amphorae. The conquest of the Narbonnaise obviously played an important role, and it seems clear that *c.* 60 B.C. the 'frontier' set by Rome on the area over which she exercised economic control lay between the Aedui and the Helvetii: the cause of the Gallic War!

In conclusion it should be emphasized that the early Gallic Wars particularly affected western Gaul. Thus, although the pretext of the Romans' entry into Gaul was the Helvetic migrations, having established a firm boundary to the east against the Helvetii and Germanic tribes, Rome was assured of the rapid and extensive conquest of Belgic Gaul and northern Armorica (57 B.C.), then southern Armorica and Aquitaine (56 B.C.), relying on her allies in eastern Gaul, especially the Aedui and Remi. We should emphasize not only the rapidity of this intervention, which Caesar had to consolidate in 54 B.C. (insufficiently, as the general unrest in Gaul occurred in 53 B.C.), but also the absence of an attack on Arvernian territory, which Caesar does not seem to have contemplated since he wrote (*B.G.* III, 28) 'all Gaul is conquered'. The question we must ask is what were the Romans' underlying motives. Economic colonialism was obviously one, and in that case the conquest of Arvernian Gaul was unnecessary since the Saône-Rhône route, the Garonne–'seuil du Poitou' route and the Loire and Seine valleys were in the hands of the Romans, well established in the Provincia. But on the other hand one might wonder whether the reason for the hurried conquest could have been the desire to impose as quickly as possible an economic blockade on Arvernian Gaul, Rome's feared enemy since 121 B.C., or at least to neutralize her.

The administrative divisions of Roman Gaul only imperfectly reflect the cultural realities of independent Gaul, which should be considered, in any research programme, in the context of continuous development through the Bronze and Iron Ages.

BIBLIOGRAPHY

Agache, R. 1976. 'Les fermes indigènes d'époque pré-romaine et romaine dans le bassin de la Somme', *Cahiers arch. de Picardie*, iii, 117–38.

Blanchet, J. C. and Buchsenschutz, O. 1983. 'La maison de La Tène moyenne de Verberie (Oise)', in *Les Gaulois dans le nord du Bassin Parisien*, Paris, 96–126.

Bouyer, M. and Buchsenschutz, O. 1982. 'La chronologie du village celtique des arênes à Levroux (Indre)', in J. Collis, A. Duval and R. Périchon (eds.), *Le deuxième âge du Fer en Auvergne et en Forez*, Paris, 72–89.

Bretz-Mahler, D. 1970. *La civilisation de La Tène I en Champagne, le faciès marnien*, XXIIIe supplément à Gallia.

Brunaux, J.-L. and Meniel, P. 1983. 'Le sanctuaire de Gournay-sur-Aronde (Oise): structures et rites. Les animaux du sacrifice', in *Les Gaulois dans le nord du Bassin Parisien*, Paris, 165–73.

Clarke, R. R. and Hawkes, C. F. C. 1955. 'An iron anthropoid sword from Shouldham, Norfolk, with related Continental and British weapons', *P.P.S.* xxi, 198–227.

Colbert de Beaulieu, J.-B. 1973. *Traité numismatique celtique*, I: *Méthodologie des ensembles*, Paris.

Collis, J. 1976. *Defended Sites of the Late La Tène in Central and Western Europe*, B.A.R. SS 2, Oxford.

Degenne, M. and Duval, A. 1983. 'La nécropole de Breuil-le-Sec (Oise), premières observations', in *Les Gaulois dans le nord du Bassin Parisien*, Paris, 74–95, 23 fig.

Delestrée, L.-P. 1974. *La circulation monétaire gauloise dans l'ouest du Belgium après la conquête romaine: les monnaies gauloises de Bois l'Abbé*, 2 vols, Paris.

Dumasy, F. 1974. 'Les théatres ruraux des Carnutes et des Sénons', *Rev. arch. du Centre*, xiii, 196, 218.

Duval, A. 1975a. 'Civilisations des oppida et sépultures de La Tène finale en Haute-Normandie', in P.-M. Duval and V. Kruta (eds.), *L'habitat et la nécropole à l'âge du Fer en Europe occidenatale*, Paris, 37–44.

—— 1975b. 'Une tombe à char de La Tène III, Inglemare (commune de Belbeuf, Seine-Maritime)', *Arch. Atlantica*, i, 2, 147–63.

—— 1976. 'Aspects de La Tène moyenne dans le Bassin Parisien', *Bull. S.P.F.* lxxiii, 147–483.

—— 1977. 'Deux objets pseudofiligranés de La Tène', *Antiquités Nationales*, ix, 40–4.

—— 1982. 'Autour de Vercingétorix: de l'archéologie à l'histoire économique et sociale', in J. Collis, A. Duval and R. Périchon (eds), *L'âge du Fer en Auvergne et en Forez*, Paris, 298–335.

—— forthcoming a. 'La Tène moyenne: du Bronze au Fer'.

—— forthcoming b. 'La notion de groupe régional dans la Gaule et particulièrement aux IIIe-I^e siècles avant J.C.'

Duval, A. and Blanchet, J.-C. 1976. ''Le deuxième âge du Fer en Picardie', *Rev. arch. de l'Oise*, vii, 48–58.

Duval, A. and Buchsenschutz, O. 1976. 'L'âge du Fer dans le Bassin Parisien et le nord de la France', in J. Guilaine (ed.), *La préhistoire française*, II: *Les civilisations néolithiques et protohistoriques de la France*, C.N.R.S., 789–801.

Duval, P.-M. 1971. *Les sources de l'histoire de France*, I: *La Gaule jusqu'au milieu du Ve siècle*, 2 parts, Paris.
—— 1977. *Les Celtes*, Paris.
Fabre, G. 1952. *Les civilisations protohistoriques de l'Aquitaine*, Paris.
Flouest, J.-L. and Stead, I. 1981. *Iron Age Cemeteries in Champagne*, B.M. Occ. Pap. VI.
Giot, P.-R. 1971. 'Ombres et lumières sur la chronologie de la céramique armoricaine a l'âge du Fer', *Ann. de Bretagne*, lxxviii, 73–92.
Hatt, J.-J. and Roualet, P. 1977. 'La chronologie de La Tène en Champagne', *Rev. arch. de l'Est*, xxviii, 7–136.
Hawkes, C. F. C. and Dunning, G. C. 1930. 'The Belgae of Gaul and Britain', *Arch. J.* lxxxviii, 150–335.
Hiernard, J. 1979. 'Poitou et Vendée avant les Romains: une enquête numismatique', *Soc. d'émulation de la Vendée*, cxxvi, 45–113.
Hinout, J. and Duval, A. Forthcoming. 'Une nécropole de La Tène initiale à Oulchy (Aisne)'.
Lardy, J.-M. 1983. 'La nécropole d'Epiais-Rhus (Val-d'Oise). Approche chronostratigraphique', in *Les Gaulois dans le nord du Bassin Parisien*, Paris, 127–58.
Mariën, M. 1961. *La période de La Tène en Belgique, le groupe de La Haine*, Brussels.
Mohen, J.-P. 1979. 'La présence celtique dans le sud-ouest de l'Europe', in P.-M. Duval and V. Kruta (eds.), *Les mouvements celtiques du Ve au I^e siècles avant notre ère*, C.N.R.S., 29–48.
Thénot, A. 1982. *La civilisation celtique dans l'est de la France*, 2 vols., Paris.
Tyers, P. 1980. 'Correspondance entre la céramique commune de La Tène III du sud-est de l'Angleterre et du nord de la France', *Septentrion*, xliv, 61–70.
Wheeler, M. and Richardson, K. M. 1957. *Hill Forts of Northern France*, Soc. Antiq. London Res. Rep. XIX.

The Basis of Contact between Britain and Gaul in the Late Pre-Roman Iron Age

Daphne Nash, F.S.A.

For the purpose of the present discussion, Britain and adjacent areas of northern Gaul may be divided into two major regions. The western region consists of Armorica and south-western Britain, and the eastern region of Belgic Gaul and south-eastern Britain. During the first century B.C. the frontier between these regions ran to the south of the Seine on the Continent, and north-westwards from the Isle of Wight in Britain. On both sides of the Channel, the western and eastern regions were culturally and socially separate, and this is reflected in most aspects of the archaeological record. Contact between them seems consequently to have been that of alien regions of similar standing: there is little evidence for the one-way cultural influence characteristic of markedly unequal regions. Both regions were, however, subdivided by the Channel into a stronger, or core, area on the Continent, and a weaker, or peripheral, area in Britain, and each of the four areas thus defined possessed its own distinctive internal organization. Although, therefore, there is clear evidence of systematic Continental influence upon southern Britain, the two British areas were politically quite separate from their Continental counterparts. It is the purpose of this paper to examine the basis of the relationship between Gaul and southern Britain in the wider perspective of the connection between both areas and the Mediterranean. It will be argued that there were important differences in the ways in which the two Continental core areas related to their respective British peripheries, linked to different roles in the long-range supply of goods and services to the Mediterranean, and that these differences had a considerable influence upon the development of southern Britain in the Late Pre-Roman Iron Age.[1]

Core-periphery relations

In certain respects, relations between weaker and stronger societies were everywhere very similar. At the level of their internal structure, stronger, or core, communities drew dependent human labour and a great variety of raw materials from weaker peripheral ones, using them to strengthen their already privileged position within their own society. In return, core communities supplied weaker ones with a range of appropriate luxury goods, and generally exercised a profound cultural influence over them, most marked at the level of peripheral social élites or nobilities. Such relationships may be observed within each of the four areas here under consideration.

Similarly, entire societies might interact as unequal partners. On this scale, a dominant or core society, through the agency of its leading communities, drew human labour and raw materials, or finished goods of relatively low social value, from the core communities of weaker ones, which may by virtue of their subordinate relationship be defined as peripheral to them. Core societies for their part supplied their peripheral counterparts with luxury and prestige goods upon which their recipients placed the highest social value of all. By the same token, the leading communities of core societies exercised a powerful political and cultural influence upon their peripheral partners. This was generally expressed by the latter's adoption from the stronger society of a range of exotic materials and cultural practices which they found especially appropriate to their own domestic concerns and traditions. Such a relationship may be observed in the Late Iron Age between Armorican Gaul and the leading communities of south-western Britain on the one hand, and between Belgic Gaul and those of eastern Britain on the other. By far the most characteristic product of a successful unequal relationship between adjacent societies was, however, the political growth of the core communities of both.

The most significant types of interaction between any two separate societies, whatever their relative standing, were therefore generally conducted at the level of their respective core communities, whose rulers used the prestige and material rewards from successful foreign relationships to increase their societies' advantage over their regional peripheries. Three types of interaction may be singled out as especially significant in this respect. The first is diplomatic contact, on the basis of which longer-term relationships of a trading or military nature might be based. Diplomatic contact involved the exchange of agreements and gifts, and sometimes an official marriage or exchange of hostages, always at the highest social level. Much of the importance which attached to the maintenance of foreign diplomatic ties undoubtedly stemmed from the political advantage which these conferred upon both parties to an agreement when managing their own domestic affairs.[2]

The second important type of external interaction was the exchange of goods and services. Two types of transaction under this heading were of particular significance. The first was trade in merchandise at places specially designated for such dealings among foreigners. In regions whose leading communities' access to exotic materials depended heavily upon trading activity, great importance was undoubtedly attached to the maintenance of privileged diplomatic relations with significant partners, under cover of which specialized trade might be conducted, and rulers of core communities might strive to establish what amounted to a trading monopoly with them. In these areas, permanent ports of foreign trade were a prominent feature of the settlement hierarchy, on political frontiers, coasts and inland waterways, and the most important ports were generally connected very closely with centres of political power. It seems that this was the dominant type of external relationship in Armorican Gaul and south-western Britain. The second important type of foreign-exchange relationship was the employment by strong authorities of warriors from weaker ones as retainers or mercenaries. This relationship is not generally reflected directly in the surviving settlement record of either participant society, but may be revealed in distinctive patterns of coinage distribution, and seems to be in evidence between Belgic Gaul and south-eastern Britain (below).

The third type of interaction among separate societies took the form of military raids or wars of conquest. This was the leading type of foreign relationship of a warrior society, and was usually combined with exchange relations which had a strong military component, particularly the sale of plunder or military services. This was characteristic of the foreign relations of the communities of Belgic Gaul and south-eastern Britain. The territorial expansion of a successful warrior society could substantially modify the political structure of its external environment when it involved colonial settlement at a distance from the expanding heartlands, and this process is illustrated by Belgic expansion into south-eastern Britain during the Late Iron Age.

Within the overall regional structure of Iron Age Gaul and Britain, therefore, the character and outlook of the core communities of each region was of paramount importance. The forces which brought each of these regional cores into systematic relationships with one another were of a lasting character despite continual changes in their fortunes, and therefore also great fluctuations in their demands upon their respective peripheries. This is because their interaction was based upon the transmission of materials and services which were, for social or environmental reasons, not available from within their own confines, and were continually consumed or passed on to others by their recipients, so that they needed constant replacement from their original sources. Short-range contact based upon recurrent mutual needs consequently bound all the regions of Iron Age Europe to their neighbours, and linked them in turn with the Mediterranean.

The cities of the north-western Mediterranean therefore stood at the core of western Europe as a whole, and exercised a profound influence upon its development. Their complex political systems and immense expenditure upon warfare, civic construction, and ruling-class display imposed a constant drain upon the human and material resources of their European hinterland, while manufactured goods of Mediterranean origin came to play a vital role in élite consumption and display throughout Iron Age Europe. The Mediterranean cities regarded temperate Europe as a boundless reservoir of raw materials, foodstuffs, and human labour, while, in the eyes of its northern periphery, the Mediterranean seemed to possess inexhaustible stores of wealth.

The Mediterranean cities' enduring need for raw materials and foodstuffs is well known and well documented. It seems likely that it was the metals of western Europe that first attracted the attentions of eastern Mediterranean sea traders, inaugurating systematic trading contact with coastal areas of the north-western Mediterranean during the ninth and eighth centuries. The need for metals and many other materials, including an increasingly wide range of foodstuffs, grew in proportion throughout the Iron Age, and exercised an important influence upon the development of most areas of Gaul and Britain.[3]

Mediterranean demand for human labour was also of great antiquity, and took two principal forms: the hire of mercenary soldiers and the purchase of slaves.[4] These needs imposed distinctive constraints upon the societies which met them, since they placed a strong emphasis upon the development of their military capacities, whether to capture slaves in raids upon weaker societies, or to earn mercenary pay and rich plunder in Mediterranean wars by supplying skilled armies of warriors. Mediterranean demand both for slaves and for mercenary soldiers therefore had a decisive influence upon the expansion of the warrior societies of temperate Europe, since these societies already relied very heavily upon the exploitation of their military capacities for access to the most important forms of exotic wealth, as will be argued below. Mercenary employment in the Mediterranean played a key role in Celtic expansion during the fifth to third centuries, while the supply of slaves to the Roman empire seems to have been an important influence upon Belgic expansion during the second and first.

The influence of the Mediterranean was of course felt most acutely by those societies with which it had the closest dealings. Each relay in the chain of contact between the Mediterranean and northern Europe diminished the immediacy of Mediterranean influence, and this is reflected in the relatively less-developed economic and political systems of the outer reaches of the European periphery when compared with areas close to the Mediterranean. The indirect effects of Mediterranean needs were nonetheless experienced even in these remote outer areas, whenever some element in recurrent interregional exchanges took on an exceptional significance because of its value in long-range systems of exchange leading towards the Mediterranean.[5] When this occurred, privileged management of the transactions in question furnished the basis for political expansion in peripheral societies.

Within the network of regions linking northern Europe with the Mediterranean, a number of distinct long-range systems can be discerned, whose disposition was influenced by the economic pull of the Mediterranean. Two such systems connected the markets of the western Mediterranean with their remote periphery in Britain, and these were divided in their outer reaches by the frontier which separated the warrior societies of Belgic Gaul from the more sedentary Celts of Armorica. These two long-range systems will be considered in more detail below, and in what follows I shall argue that the social basis of contact between Britain and Gaul, and therefore the basis on which goods and services were transmitted between them, differed in significant respects between the western and eastern regions, so that each made a different but complementary contribution to the economy of stronger Continental regions and ultimately to the Mediterranean.

Two types of Celtic society

Celtic societies everywhere may be described as agrarian, meaning that their subsistence was based upon compatriot agricultural labour. Each community was therefore in principle self-supporting. Since, however, no social territory was wholly self-sufficient even in the necessities for its bare subsistence, goods not available from within its own resources were acquired through a range of social and economic exchanges based upon the systematic production of a material surplus. Such exchanges might take place, for instance, in the course of reciprocal hospitality at household level, or at periodic agricultural fairs at community level.[6] Short-range mutual trade with external communities in foodstuffs and essential raw materials was an extension of this activity and, although it came under overall political supervision, its commonplace character meant that it had a relatively modest influence upon most societies' social development.

Compatriot peasant labour was at the same time the foundation of noble wealth. Peasants' agricultural produce and labour services contributed to the support of the nobility through customary dues, tax and rent, while their military services were employed for the defence or enlargement of territories, and to conduct disputes with rival nobles or external neighbours; warfare was also in most societies a useful source of windfall revenue in the form of spoils, ransom and indemnity payments, and could lead to long-term revenues in the form of tribute from defeated opponents.

An important component of noble wealth was therefore provided by revenues and services from free compatriot peasants, and the way in which they were obtained gave each society its distinctive economic orientation. This was, however, not sufficient to sustain a developed political economy, and was in consequence supplemented by the produce and labour of slaves, dependent craftsmen, resident foreigners and non-compatriot tributary dependants. Revenues from these sources were of vital importance if political expansion was to take place. Noble revenues which were not directly consumed were mainly converted into higher forms of wealth by customary exchange associated with mutual hospitality and diplomatic agreements, and by negotiated trade with external societies, all of which gave access to, politically, the most significant categories of wealth.

All Celtic societies seem therefore to have possessed this basic agrarian economic structure. Customary contractual ties among kin groups played an important role in articulating all internal economic relationships, and gave rise everywhere to very similar political formations. There were, however, two distinct variant forms of Celtic agrarian society, distinguished by the predominant way in which compatriot peasant labour was transformed into social wealth, and these may for convenience be termed (purely) agrarian and warrior (agrarian) respectively. The conditions which influenced whether a particular Celtic society developed along a purely agrarian path or as a warrior society remain a matter for speculation, but two considerations may be isolated as being of especial significance. The first was the physical character of its geographical environment, since this was the ultimate source of its livelihood and was an influence on whether its own material production was capable of supporting political expansion. The second was the nature of the demands made upon it by its most prestigious and rewarding foreign associates, since exotic goods acquired from them played a key role in the exercise of political power. Successful relations with foreign markets, whether for merchandise or for military labour, tended in consequence to reinforce the internal social commitments of the society which supplied what they required.

Regions close to the Mediterranean, and therefore exposed to the strongest external demands, were obliged to make the clearest commitment to one or other path of internal development. Remoter regions exposed to less rewarding but also less exacting external relations generally also possessed less complex political systems, which imposed lighter burdens upon their producing populations. These were not necessarily obliged to adopt an exclusive commitment to one particular form of internal social organization and might possess less clearly differentiated political economies. They might accordingly preserve both types of productive practice in more balanced proportions, or oscillate between them as alternatives.[7] As these societies were drawn more closely into the orbit of the Mediterranean, however, they tended to develop a more specialized economy in response to the specific external circumstances in which they then found themselves. By the first century, Armorica and Belgic Gaul had developed far along their separate paths, ultimately influenced by their different contributions to long-range European procurement networks for slave labour and raw materials. Environmental as well as social differences therefore played an important role in their separate development, and their relations with their respective British peripheries were in consequence also differently based. This contact in turn influenced the divergent development of south-western and south-eastern Britain in the Late Iron Age.

Purely agrarian societies

Purely agrarian societies, characteristic of Armorican Gaul and south-western Britain, were those in which agricultural produce, raw materials and finished goods produced within a society itself both by free peasants and by dependent labour were the principal basis of its social wealth. This primary surplus was transformed into more valuable forms of wealth mainly by exchange, and internal marketing systems tended to develop early under noble supervision, ultimately encouraging large-scale craft production for exchange, which soon assumed an important role not only in domestic but also in external trading activity. Exogenous wealth, by the same token, was mainly derived from the profits of trade with external partners. Domestic manufactured goods and a small quantity of more valuable exotica were traded to weaker societies for raw materials and slaves; of these, some were consumed and the rest, together with appropriate types of domestic agricultural and mineral surplus, were traded to stronger societies for more valuable types of exotic goods.

This pattern of external contact placed a heavy emphasis upon a society's ability to supply specific merchandise to its various trading partners, and tin, silver, copper and gold were of prime importance in linking the metalliferous areas of western Britain with Armorican Gaul, and ultimately with Mediterranean markets in Languedoc (below). These metals, required not only in the Mediterranean but by most other Continental societies as well, were most abundant in their raw state in the western regions of Gaul and Britain, prompting their exploitation as a resource which could be traded profitably to outsiders. This economic commitment, however, made heavy demands upon agricultural labour and craftsmen, since the producing population had not only to support the society at its accustomed level of affluence, but to produce the materials necessary to sustain profitable foreign relationships as well. These archetypal agrarian societies therefore always possessed a large and heavily exploited producing population, and avoided undue mobilization of this population as soldiers, since military commitments interfered with its productive concerns. Warfare could not therefore serve the same social and economic functions as it did in a warrior society.[8]

In a purely agrarian society, therefore, the nobility was militarily active and fiercely competitive among itself, assisted by skilled warriors from among the richest strata of the peasantry, who alone had a regular military function.[9] Military force was, however, employed mainly for the defence or enlargement of political territories, the policing of tributaries, and for the conduct of disputes among neighbouring nobilities, not for wars of extensive foreign conquest or for systematic plundering raids. Warfare in these societies was never a dependable source of external revenues. The expansion of chiefdoms or states of this type was therefore largely a domestic affair, concerned with the progressive extension of control over a widening circle of weaker neighbours, and the tightening of political control within the core territory of the society itself. When such societies used a coinage, as in the first century in Armorica and south-western Britain, this political characteristic is reflected in the confinement of each coinage to a relatively well-defined territory within which it was probably used in a continuous cycle of internal official payments and taxation; such coinages seldom strayed far from their territory of origin, since they played no significant role in the conduct of external relationships.[10]

The developed settlement pattern of such a society betrays its productive concerns. Rulers whose prosperity depended upon their ability to provide for and supervise the distribution and exchange of goods within their own territories and with the outside world tended to form major nucleated settlements of very distinctive form, with both political and economic functions. These settlements needed access to a varied immediate hinterland, and the strongest also tended to dominate long-range lines of communication with external territories and were generally linked very closely with a port of foreign trade. They were therefore often located on the interface of several different ecological zones, and at key points on important river systems. They were also centres of manufacturing activity, perhaps performed by dependants of the ruling house, and possessed storage facilities associated with their distributional functions. Their political importance is revealed by their close association with the production and use of coinage, and they were themselves often a prime object of noble expenditure. Some, for instance, were adorned with multiple ramparts whose construction made extravagant use of human labour and reveal a concern as much with ostentatious display as with defence.[11]

Internal settlements of this type seem generally to have been the principal seats of political power in the purely agrarian societies of western Gaul and Britain, whose rulers' overriding concern in their external relationships was to maintain the peaceful negotiated agreements with foreign partners under the terms of which profitable trade could be conducted. Ports of trade on or near political boundaries, where visiting traders could be entertained and goods manufactured or assembled for exchange on the spot or for shipment elsewhere, were consequently a prominent feature of the settlement record of such a society, since they performed a vital economic function for its ruling nobility. In coastal areas, these generally formed around a good harbour easily accessible from the leading settlements in their hinterland, and one which for geographical reasons alien ships might almost be compelled to put into. Like Hengistbury Head or Alet, such ports might attract a large resident population and become major settlements in their own right.

Warrior agrarian societies

The second variant form of Celtic society was the warrior societies which dominate the ancient sources because of their impact upon Mediterranean consciousness. These were characteristic of Belgic Gaul and south-eastern Britain. Here, peasants' labour as such was the most important source of social wealth from the compatriot community, appropriated by the nobility by means of contractual and military relationships. In common with purely agrarian societies, they possessed an agrarian subsistence economy, but supervised distributional or marketing activity dependent upon the production of a material surplus played a negligible role in the conversion of free compatriot peasant labour into higher forms of wealth. Internal marketing systems were in consequence poorly developed, and mainly supported the subsistence economy by allowing for the interchange of resources unequally distributed in the natural environment.[12] Manufactured goods and wealth items were instead distributed primarily as gifts, grants and payments associated with customary and contractual relations with the noble houses who maintained craftsmen, had access to exotica, and provided military leadership. It was, therefore, mainly in service for personal overlords that peasants acquired the wealth goods they needed, and those which were obtained in the course of military service, as payment, reward, or share of the plunder, were of especial significance. The conditions under which wealth goods were distributed in a warrior society therefore probably account for the plainly élite and military character of much craft production within them; large-scale production of more commonplace manufactured goods for internal distribution or external trade was comparatively slow to develop.

In warrior societies, therefore, access to the exogenous wealth required for political expansion was based upon contact with external societies which had a strong military component. This contact may be divided into two categories: offensive warfare, and negotiated exchange. Offensive warfare against weaker and stronger societies alike enabled a warrior nobility to employ peasant military labour to exploit external societies directly. Where relations with peripheral societies were concerned, greater revenues were obtained as spoils, ransom and military indemnities than as profits of negotiated trade in merchandise, while plundering stronger societies yielded unpredictable but often very great rewards.[13] Offensive warfare was also employed to obtain foreign land by conquest, and to acquire and police external tributaries. Owing to the rather low level of domestic surplus production in most warrior societies, tribute from dependent external societies was of critical importance as a source of surplus revenues both for consumption and for foreign trade.

Negotiated exchange as a source of social wealth took two forms. The first and most important was external trade with stronger societies in plunder, particularly human captives, and in produce from tributaries and compatriot dependants. Domestic produce, perhaps especially animal products, played a modest role in such exchanges; far more important were the tribute and plunder obtained from outside the compatriot community more or less directly as an outcome of offensive warfare. Such trade enabled warrior societies to obtain reliable supplies of luxury manufactured goods and exotic drink, and was conducted either with visiting traders on the frontiers of warrior territory itself, or at foreign markets in alien regions. Warriors with merchandise to sell might on occasion travel long distances to appropriate markets.[14] It is likely that the warrior societies of south-eastern Britain related to the agrarian societies of the south-west in this way, as did the Continental Belgae to the markets of Armorica and eastern Gaul (below).

The second form of negotiated external relationship involved the exchange of a weaker warrior society's military labour for wealth goods, entertainment and military service from a stronger one. This was an extremely rewarding form of external relationship for both partners. It provided dependent warriors not only with the customary fruits of offensive warfare in what was often a richer region, but also with payment, commonly in the form of gold coinage, with the prestige of association with the rulers of a stronger society, and with opportunities to develop their military skills, an important objective in its own right. At the same time it enabled the employer of mercenary armies or dependent allies to exploit their often very considerable military expertise in pursuit of his own political ends. Any strong and wealthy society might hire Celtic mercenaries. Service in Mediterranean armies undoubtedly first introduced the Celts to the use of precious-metal coinage during the fourth and third centuries, while I shall argue that British military service for Belgic overlords accounts for the introduction of Belgic gold coinage into Britain during the second and first centuries.

These offensive and negotiated relations with stronger external societies were therefore a warrior society's principal source of exogenous luxury and prestige goods, and profitable foreign dealings on this basis served strongly to reinforce a successful warrior society's internal social orientation. Warrior societies therefore generally maintained a high level of military mobilization among the compatriot peasant population, and this had an impact upon their material culture. Noble wealth was invested less in the embellishment of households and settlements and the support of manufacturing and trading activity, than in the effort to attract, entertain and protect dependants of all ranks, and to prepare for military enterprises, since these served the economic functions performed by production for exchange in purely agrarian societies. A relatively greater emphasis was therefore placed upon the development of readily distributable forms of moveable wealth such as metal goods and livestock, and craftsmen's skills were employed above all to manufacture weapons, payment goods and the paraphernalia of display and feasting associated with noble rivalry to attract and maintain dependants, retainers and mercenaries. In these societies, gold coinage was almost certainly struck and distributed primarily as a means of payment for compatriot and foreign warriors. Where foreign mercenaries were employed on a recurrent short-term basis, this often results in a very different pattern of coinage distribution from that observed in a purely agrarian society since, under these circumstances, much coinage permanently left its territory of origin with warriors returning to their native communities. Such a pattern may arguably be observed in the distribution of Belgic gold coinage in Britain (Nash forthcoming c).

A warrior economy also affected a society's use of territory, since pressing military demands upon men of productive age during peak seasons of the agricultural year meant that such societies often developed the less labour-intensive but territorially more demanding pastoral sector at the expense of intensive arable cultivation. The accumulation of herds, not simply for subsistence but as an important form of wealth necessary for articulating contractual relations among compatriots, helps to account for the prevalence within warrior territories of uninhabited defensive enclosures suitable for the husbandry of livestock and its protection from rustling.

The overall settlement pattern of an agrarian warrior society in its purest form, as in parts of Belgic Gaul and south-eastern Britain, therefore reflects very clearly its peculiar social and economic commitments. Weakly developed internal marketing systems inhibited the development of craft production for distribution and exchange, and nucleated settlements with clearly defined distributional functions are therefore lacking. The largest noble settlements in a warrior society were instead in all likelihood the inflated households of the dominant nobility, attached to their estates, and might take the form of rambling establishments with internal pasturage for sheep, cattle and horses, and space for the accommodation of variable numbers of dependants and visitors.[15] Ports of foreign trade, where they existed at all, were no more than formal and externalized points of contact with the outside world, where merchandise was assembled for exchange. Those on the frontiers of a purely warrior territory seldom if ever attracted a large resident population, or supported extensive manufacturing activity, being peripheral to the domestic political and economic concerns of the society on whose margins they stood.[16]

This internal economic structure was well adapted to the geographical environment of the Celtic north, particularly the Seine basin, Picardy and south-eastern Britain, which in contrast with the west possessed few scarce and marketable natural resources capable of supporting political expansion based primarily upon the exchange of a society's own produce. Instead, the leading societies of northern Gaul and eastern Britain seem throughout the Iron Age to have developed their military capacities to secure the exogenous wealth they required, so that they became both a dependable source of captured slaves, and prime suppliers of skilled mercenary soldiers for stronger societies willing to employ them.

Politically, warrior societies were prone to develop intolerable internal tensions because of the large military component in noble competition, and this, together with their unusually demanding territorial needs, their need to accumulate numerous tributary dependants to sustain their economy, and their overriding concern to engage in regular offensive warfare, meant that a period of political growth was almost by definition also one of substantial territorial expansion, frequently in the form of foreign colonization. The expansion of these societies therefore took a rather different form from that of their more sedentary agrarian counterparts. Their need to collect external tributaries was if anything more pressing because of their limited internal productive capacity, and this could lead to the formation of extensive but unstable political groupings.[17] Nobility and warrior-peasants alike required freehold land, and this need, backed by force, could not indefinitely be met within a pre-existing territory. The political tensions generated by an ambitious and successful warrior nobility were therefore most commonly resolved by the conquest and settlement of foreign land, and colonial emigration is a prominent feature of political growth in a warrior society, well exemplified by Belgic expansion into southern Britain during the Late Iron Age. Foreign colonization generally followed the path of existing external contacts: in a peripheral direction it followed and supported raiding activity, while in a core-wards direction it approached its principal external markets, particularly those for mercenary labour.

Britain and Gaul

Where Britain and adjacent areas of Gaul are concerned, therefore, the pattern of contact during the Late Pre-Roman Iron Age rested upon these different social foundations. In the western zone, a chain of external trading contact founded upon participant regions' own production linked Roman provincial territory in south-western Gaul with south-western Britain (Cunliffe 1982). Italian traders from Narbo therefore brought wine and other Mediterranean produce to native markets on the provincial frontier, where they were probably exchanged for a wide range of foodstuffs, and for merchandise which native provincial traders had assembled from their own sources inside and outside the province. These goods undoubtedly included metals from the Massif Central and Atlantic Gaul, and slaves mainly purchased from warrior communities nearby in south-western Gaul and Aquitania.[18] A further relay, probably under the management of provincial traders or autonomous communities close to the Roman frontier, then brought wine to Bordeaux or overland to central Gaul and Armorica.[19] The maritime route between Bordeaux and western Armorica seems to have assumed increasing importance during the second and first centuries, and was probably mainly under the management of the Veneti, who brought Armorican and British metals and raw materials south to Bordeaux where they could obtain wine for trade with Atlantic communities on their homeward journeys, and for their own consumption on arrival.[20] Within Armorica itself, therefore, much wine acquired by both maritime and landwards routes was consumed, but a proportion was re-exported in a final relay which linked the Coriosolites and Venelli of northern Armorica with south-western Britain; the importance of this link was probably based upon the Armorican communities' own need for British metals, and the additional value which some of these metals possessed as a component in their southwards trade for wine.

In Armorica, consequently, the strongest, or core, communities were those which occupied key positions on the coast from which sea trade could be controlled: the Veneti, who seem likely to have dominated southwards trade and were strongest of all; the Osismi of Finistère, who may have had independent links with the south-western British peninsula (Cunliffe 1982, 61); and the Coriosolites and Venelli on the northern coast, who seem to have had privileged management of the most rewarding of all trade with Britain, especially from the Coriosolitan port of Alet. In Britain, similarly, the Durotriges seem to have held the key position, with a dominant port at Hengistbury Head (Cunliffe 1978; 1982; Mays 1981). Here, metals from Wales, the Mendips and the Cornish peninsula could be assembled for exchange with Armorican traders, together with Durotrigian domestic produce such as iron, and probably also slaves and animal products purchased from the warrior communities of south-eastern Britain.

Significant and regular contact between the inhabitants of Armorica and Britain was almost certainly, therefore, confined to major coastal settlements. In Britain these were mainly in what Cunliffe (1982, 48, 63) has termed the Wessex contact zone, although Continental ships may well have put into ports and harbours elsewhere along the Channel coasts of Britain, dealing in goods of relatively less value than those involved in the primary transactions at the principal Durotrigian ports. There is no reason to suspect colonial settlement from Armorica anywhere on the coast of Britain, and in this respect relations between Britain and the Continent differed markedly in the two zones of contact.

In the eastern zone, a different economic chain linked south-eastern Britain with Mediterranean markets in the lower Rhône valley and northern Italy. Here, provincial traders supplied wine and associated Mediterranean produce to native kingdoms and states immediately outside the provincial frontier in exchange for slaves and raw materials, much as happened in the west, but the long-range peripheral procurement networks which fed the native markets of eastern Gaul were different. Among their most important sources of provision were the warrior societies of northern Gaul, who supplied raw materials such as Rhineland iron, probably acquired from tributary dependants, and captives of war, sold as slaves.[21] Gallic warrior societies' ability to trade profitably in this particular merchandise was due ultimately to the Roman empire's growing need for slaves during the second and first centuries, associated with the development of the Italian wine export industry, and a general expansion of the Roman economy.

Belgic expansion during the Late Iron Age seems likely to have been closely linked with the needs of Italian slave markets, since the geographical environment of the warrior societies of the Seine basin and Picardy made them more dependent than many upon purely military sources of revenue. During the third and second centuries, the Belgic region of Gaul possessed a single outstanding core area of small but seemingly wealthy warrior chiefdoms around the watershed of the Somme, Scheldt and Sambre.[22] The gradual expansion of this core area was probably based upon its rulers' contact with the then dominant warrior chiefdoms of the middle Rhineland, perhaps especially as dependent military allies.[23] By the second century, the entire Somme valley and adjacent maritime districts seem to have been drawn into this early Belgic core.

During the second and early first century, however, the focus of Belgic expansion seems to have shifted southwards into the central Seine basin, especially around the Aisne.[24] This development appears to have been linked with the fortunes of the stronger and predominantly agrarian societies of eastern Gaul at the head of the Rhône valley, particularly the Aedui, Sequani and their neighbours, whose sudden promotion in the 120s to a position on the frontier of the Roman empire led to a phase of rapid political and economic growth. These eastern Gallic states soon displaced the old middle Rhineland chiefdoms from the position of cultural and economic dominance which they had previously held in northern Gaul, and it is probable that they provided new and rewarding markets for the produce and above all for the slaves which their Belgic neighbours in the Seine basin could supply (Nash forthcoming b). By the mid-first century, therefore, the Belgic core area may be divided into two distinct sub-regions, centred in Picardy and the Seine basin respectively.

Relations between Belgic Gaul and Britain were in turn those of a warrior core area with its corresponding periphery. Belgic contact with southern Britain was therefore not primarily based upon the pacific trading contact that was characteristic of the western zone, nor was it confined to offshore or coastal settlements. Instead, Belgic contact with Britain had a strong military component and was territorially intrusive: Caesar described both aspects when he said that British soldiers had served in 'most' Gallic wars, and that the Belgae had gone to Britain first to raid and then to settle (*B.G.* IV, 20, 1; cf. III, 9, 9; V, 12, 2). British military service for Belgic overlords both in Gaul and in Britain itself undoubtedly accounts for the large-scale importation of Belgic gold coinage into Britain during the second and first centuries, since this was arguably the staple payment for skilled warriors in most of the strongest societies of Late Iron Age Gaul.

This pattern of contact seems to have been established by the late third century between the early Belgic core area in Picardy and the British communities of northern Kent.[25] During the second and first centuries there was a well-defined area between the Thames and the Medway which had peculiarly close and abiding ties with the chiefdoms of the Somme valley, reflected in the distribution of Ambianic gold coinage. Cultural, if not political, ties seem indeed to have endured long after Caesar's conquest of Gaul, since the Kentish silver and bronze coinages of the later first century continue to imitate the repertoire of the post-conquest Ambiani.[26] This area, with its strong distributions of Belgic gold coinage and absence of an early British coinage of its own, was clearly a focus of Belgic interest and activity in Britain, and it is probably here that the oldest and most successful Belgic colonies are to be sought. These functioned not only as emigrant settlements in their own right, but as footholds from which campaigns and raids into remoter areas of Britain could be organized. Similar ties seem later to have been formed between the southern Belgic core area in the Seine basin and central-southern Britain in Sussex and Hampshire. These are reflected in the tradition of the Suessionian king Diviciacus' dominions in Britain (Caesar, *B.G.* II, 4, 7) and the ultimate adoption of a Suessionian rather than an Ambianic prototype for the native British coinages of the central and western areas.[27]

Belgic colonies in Britain probably involved a comparatively small number of nobles and warriors, but their political influence in their new homes was disproportionately great because of their ties of kinship and political affinity with the dominant Continental kingdoms from which they had sprung. This intrusion of Belgic Gaul into Britain was a phenomenon not matched in the western zone, but was characteristic of the relations between an expanding warrior society and its dependent periphery.

Successful, in the sense of politically dominant, Belgic colonies seem therefore to have been concentrated in an area to the south of the lower Thames valley, to which Caesar referred as 'most civilized' and 'most like Gaul' (*B.G.* v, 14, 1). This Belgic or Belgicized area, with its intimate political and military ties with the Continent, was surrounded in turn by a ring of resident British warrior societies in East Anglia, the Midlands and central-southern Britain. The political and economic expansion of these societies in the first century was probably founded upon dependent relations with their Belgic neighbours, who stood to them as senior allies and military leaders, and this appears to be reflected in the history of development of the earliest British gold coinages around the time of Caesar's war. By that time, the strongest warrior kingdoms of southern Britain seem likely to have attained the status of peripheral external dependencies of the dominant Belgic kingdoms, comparable with others on the Continent itself, such as the Atrebates, Nervii or Eburones (Nash forthcoming c).

Finally, it remains to consider briefly the basis of contact between the eastern and western regions of Gaul and Britain. Predominantly agrarian and warrior societies were complementary and interdependent forms of social organization, each performing functions necessary for the other's survival. Warrior societies strongly committed to a military economy, as were the leading communities of Late Iron Age Belgic Gaul and eastern Britain, were dependent upon agrarian societies for access to Mediterranean luxury goods, metals, and trade goods, while developed agrarian societies such as those of Armorica or eastern Gaul needed slaves, animal products and often also soldiers from their warrior counterparts. The sharp division between Belgic and Armorican Gaul is evident in most aspects of their very different cultural records, not least in the abrupt separation of coinage distributions at the Seine (Scheers 1977, *passim*). If these regions related to one another on any systematic basis, it was as mutually alien societies of roughly equal standing, probably on the basis of formally negotiated treaties among a relatively small number of prominent communities, under the terms of which certain categories of exchange might be conducted.

There is some slight evidence for relations of this character between northern Armorica and the Belgic coastline, and between the Durotrigian ports in Britain and the Hampshire and Sussex coast as far east as Beachy Head.[28] It is, therefore, possible, although not yet demonstrable, that some of the warrior societies of both Belgic Gaul and Britain brought plunder and produce to their respective coastlines at points convenient for trade with ships from the west, in order to obtain from them the metals and luxury goods they required for their own consumption and for trade with other external partners. The inconspicuous nature of any such places on the shores of warrior territory either side of the Channel reflects their marginal function so far as the domestic economy of Belgic Gaul and south-eastern Britain was concerned, but their existence would help to account for the wealth of the warrior communities in the immediate hinterland of every key point on both the Belgic and south-eastern British coastlines.[29]

NOTES

[1] The period here in question is the second and first centuries unless otherwise specified; all dates are b.c. This paper is based upon work which will be presented more fully in my *Lineage, Class and State in Celtic Europe c. 500–50 b.c.*, which is in preparation. For more detailed discussion of core-periphery relations in a wider geographical context see Nash (forthcoming b). For the archaeology of Armorica see Giot *et al.* 1979.

[2] An example of such an alliance is that between Augustus and 'Dumnobellaunus and Tincommius, kings of the Britons' (*Res Gestae Divi Augusti*, 32, 1; Strabo ɪv, 5, 3). The British kings thereby received gifts, political prestige and guarantees of privileged trading arrangements, while Augustus was enabled to boast of his far-flung alliances and friendship treaties.

[3] See, e.g., Clarke (1969) 1979, 317 ff.

[4] Trade with barbarians commonly involved animal products and slaves, e.g. Strabo v, 1, 8 (Aquileia and the Illyrians); ɪv, 5, 2 (Britain and Gaul); xɪ, 2, 3 (Tanaïs on the Black Sea); ɪv, 6, 2 (Genua of the Ligures). For the antiquity of this trade see Nash (forthcoming a).

[5] This was the case, for instance, with Baltic amber (Tacitus, *Germania*, xLv, 4) and probably also Atlantic tin (e.g. Strabo, ɪɪɪ, 5, 11).

[6] Thus mountain communities would exchange such goods as cheese, pitch and honey for foodstuffs from valley communities (Strabo, ɪv, 6, 9).

[7] Relatively undifferentiated economies may probably be observed in northern Britain during this period. Sometimes a shift in economic orientation occurred, as in central-southern Britain at the beginning of the second century, which may then have moved from a predominantly agrarian structure to a warrior economy, reflected in changes in settlement pattern and political outlook (cf. Cunliffe (1974) 1978, 282 f., 285). This change is probably linked with the southwards expansion

of the Belgic core area described below, drawing central-southern Britain firmly into the orbit of the warrior east.

[8] Agrarian states might rely upon mercenary warriors to supplement the levy of skilled compatriot soldiers (Caesar, *B.G.* i, 31, 4). The Arverni and Sequani of eastern Gaul, who did so, seem to have employed German rather than Belgic mercenaries, resulting in German rather than Belgic expansion into eastern Gaul.

[9] At the level of the nobility, therefore, all Celtic societies display the same preoccupation with warfare and associated pursuits, illustrated, for instance, in a universal concern with defensive enclosures, or in the military motifs on Armorican as well as Belgic coinage.

[10] For distribution maps of Iron Age coinages in Britain see Cunliffe (ed.) 1981, 62–92; for Armorica see Colbert de Beaulieu 1973, 125 (Redones), 127 (Corisolites); Gruel 1981, 9 (Coriosolites).

[11] For such sites in Britain see, e.g., Cunliffe (1974) 1978, 273, 281 f. For the principles governing their location see, e.g., Frankenstein and Rowlands 1978.

[12] Internal marketing systems were not inherently incompatible with a warrior economy, but were not an intrinsic feature, and seem only to have developed strongly when such a society, for whatever reason, had instituted a mixed economy.

[13] Caesar recognized this when he invited all comers to plunder the Belgic Eburones on his behalf (*B.G.* vi, 34, 8).

[14] Cf. Caesar, *B.G.* iv, 2, 1 on German trade in spoils of war. The tradition that the Belgae would not admit traders in wine or Mediterranean luxury goods (*B.G.* ii, 15, 4, cf. i, 1, 3) does not necessarily mean that they engaged in no foreign trade, but probably indicated a preference for taking their own merchandise to external markets, which enabled them to exercise discretion over what was imported into their territories (cf. Wells 1980, 136 f. for similar trade at an earlier period).

[15] The largest such settlements in Britain belong to the latest phase of the Iron Age in the first century A.D., and include Selsey, Venta, Calleva, Bagendon, Verulamium and Camulodunum (Cunliffe (1974) 1978, 100–14).

[16] This observation does not necessarily hold true in areas with a mixed or colonial economy.

[17] Such, for instance, was Cunobelinus' kingdom, and probably also the dominant Belgic grouping in Picardy during the second century (Nash forthcoming c). For fuller treatment of foreign colonization see Nash (forthcoming a, b).

[18] This was the wine sent 'to the enemy' and conveyed over level plains to slave markets apparently outside the Province (Cicero, *Pro Fonteio*, 9, 19; Diodorus Siculus, v, 26, 3).

[19] The economic expansion of the first-century kingdoms of the Garonne basin, many of which were allied to, or 'friends' of, Rome, must surely be connected with an important role in the transmission of trade goods between the Roman province and remoter areas of Gaul.

[20] There is little evidence to suggest that Roman rather than native shipping dominated this Atlantic trade before the mid-first century; the subsequent replacement of native by Roman merchantmen may have had much to do with the relative peripheralization of Armorica after the conquest, having lost its autonomous function in the conveyance of long-range Atlantic trade.

[21] For Rhineland iron see, e.g., Piggott (1965, 246). The best-documented trade of this type was that with the client kingdom of Noricum (Alföldy 1974), conducted between Italian traders from Aquileia and the kings of Noricum at the Magdalensberg (cf. Strabo, v, 1, 8). For pre-Caesarian trade through the Alps see, e.g., Caesar, *B.G.* iii, 1, 2; Strabo, iv, 6, 6–7. The distribution of Roman wine amphorae and Campanian ware in the territory of Roman allies and 'friends' in eastern Gaul suggests a similar economic relationship (Peacock 1971; Nash 1978, 112–13).

[22] The best evidence for their existence at present is their coinage (Scheers 1977, 219–28). An early coastal grouping at the mouth of the Somme is also in evidence (Scheers 1977, 234–5).

[23] This relationship may be inferred firstly from their geographical location, and secondly from their presumed third-century contact with Tarentum (Scheers 1968), almost certainly via the Rhine and Adriatic, a corridor familiar also to the iron-supplying chiefdoms of the middle Rhineland. I am indebted to Michael Rowlands and John Taylor for valuable discussion of this subject.

[24] Once more this is best illustrated in their coinages, e.g. Scheers 1977, 311 and fig. 128, but is also reflected in the historical tradition of Suessionian power during the generation before Caesar (*B.G.* ii, 4, 7).

[25] For coin distributions see Cunliffe (ed.) 1981, 62–3, 65, 67; for further discussion see Nash (forthcoming c).

[26] E.g. Dubnovellaunus: Mack 1975, 286, cf. Scheers 1977 fig. 390; Mack 291, cf. Scheers fig. 396.

[27] Suessionian prototype: Scheers 1977, 365–73 and pl. VII, 174–6; British Q: Allen 1961, pl. x, 58–61; Cunliffe (ed.) 1981, 71.

[28] The principal evidence lies in coinage distributions, e.g. Gallo-Belgic D: in Gaul, Scheers 1977, 297–307; in Britain, Cunliffe (ed.) 1981, 66. A community of interest among the coastal societies of Gaul is suggested by patterns of political alliance, e.g. Caesar, *B.G.* III, 9, 9.

[29] For coin distributions in Gaul see Scheers 1977, 234–5, 259 (Ambiani), 287 (Caleti), 302 ('Morini', = Gallo-Belgic D), 363 (Veliocasses). In Britain the area from the Isle of Wight to Beachy Head was comparable (Cunliffe (ed.) 1981, 66–8, 70–1, 75); Selsey Bill is likely to have been the most important eastern port of call.

BIBLIOGRAPHY

Alföldy, G. 1974. *Noricum*, London.

Allen, D. F. 1961. 'The origins of coinage in Britain: a reappraisal', in S. S. Frere (ed.), *Problems of the Iron Age in Southern Britain*, London, 97–308.

Clarke, D. L. (1969) 1979. 'The economic context of trade and industry in barbarian Europe till Roman times', in *Analytical Archaeologist* (ed. his colleagues), London, 263–331.

Colbert de Beaulieu, J.-B. 1973. *Traité de numismatique celtique*, I, Paris.

Cunliffe, B. W. (1974) 1978. *Iron Age Communities in Britain*, London, 2nd edn.

—— 1978. *Hengistbury Head*, London.

—— 1981. (Ed.). *Coinage and Society in Britain and Gaul*, C.B.A. Res. Rep. 38, London.

—— 1982. 'Britain, the Veneti and beyond', *Oxford J. Arch.* i, 1, 39–68.

Frankenstein, S. and Rowlands, M. J. 1978. 'The internal structure and regional context of Early Iron Age society in south-western Germany', *Inst. of Arch. Bulletin*, xv, London, 73–112.

Giot, P.-R., Briard, J. and Pape, L. 1979. *Protohistoire de la Bretagne*, Rennes.

Gruel, K. 1981. *Le trésor de Trébry (Côtes-du-Nord)*, Paris.

Hill, D. and Jesson, M. 1971. *The Iron Age and its Hill-Forts*, Southampton.

Mack, R. P. 1975. *The Coinage of Ancient Britain*, London, 3rd edn.

Mays, M. 1981. 'Strabo IV, 4, 1: a reference to Hengistbury Head?', *Antiquity*, lv, 55–7.

Nash, D. 1978. *Settlement and Coinage in Central Gaul c. 200–50 B.C.*, B.A.R. S 39, Oxford.

—— forthcoming a. 'Celtic territorial expansion and the Mediterranean world', in T. Champion and V. Megaw (eds.), *Settlement and Society: Aspects of Western European Prehistory in the First Millennium B.C.*, Leicester.

—— forthcoming b. 'Core and periphery in the western European Iron Age', in M. Rowlands, M. Larsen and K. Christiansen (eds.), *Core and Periphery in the Ancient World*, Cambridge.

—— forthcoming c. 'Reflections on the origins of coinage in Britain', *Oxford J. Arch.*

Peacock, D. P. S. 1971. 'Roman amphorae in pre-Roman Britain', in Hill and Jesson 1971, 161–188.

Piggott, S. 1965. *Ancient Europe*, Edinburgh.

Scheers, S. 1968. 'Le premier monnayage des Ambiani', *Revue belge de numismatique*, cxiv, 45–73.

—— 1977. *Traité de numismatique celtique*, II: *La Gaule belgique*, Paris.

Wells, P. S. 1980. *Culture Contact and Culture Change: Early Iron Age Central Europe and the Mediterranean World*, Cambridge.

Concluding Remarks

Pierre-Roland Giot, Hon.F.S.A.

Each contribution to this collection of seminar papers contains a wealth of facts and interpretations, which I do not feel I should attempt to summarize here in any general way. If we set aside Alain Duval's exposition of regional groups in western France, Dr. Stead's is the only paper which deals in part with a period earlier than the latest Pre-Roman Iron Age and, as the author admits, his conclusions have been somewhat negative, ruling out objects as imports rather than discovering new ones. So the contributors have confined themselves to a very short chronological period—short, that is, from the point of view of the prehistorian, or even the historian taking a long view.

The relative importance of the mid-Channel sea-routes and those across the Straits of Dover has been considered by most of the contributors: the western routes are now seen as somewhat less important economically than previously supposed. And yet in the Dark Ages the western routes were considered short. Procopius (VIII, 20, 55) speaks of journeys lasting a day and a night. The *Vita* of St. Hervé (*Herveus*) states: *brevis est transitus maris inter nostrum Domnoniam et ulteriorem Britanniam*. In the eleventh century, Adam of Bremen (*Gesta Hammaburgensis Ecclesiae Ponticum*) states: *de Prol* [i.e. Prawle Point, Devon] *in Britanniam, ad sanctum Mathiam uno die* . . .. (I am indebted to Professor L. Fleuriot for the benefit of his erudition.)

The different roles of the various Armorican tribes in boat-building and navigation are still obscure: I have always believed that the Osismi have been underestimated from this point of view.

Perhaps undue emphasis has been placed on amphorae because of their better survival value. They may be no more representative of contacts than coins or metalwork, and in our speculation on the nature of trade in this period we must bear in mind that we lack evidence for the precise quantities and range of goods transported across the Channel in either direction. We need more information on the actual size and densities of population in the various geographical regions.

It remains to the Chairman to thank Professor B. W. Cunliffe for suggesting the theme of the seminar, the President of the Society of Antiquaries, Professor C. N. L. Brooke, and the staff, notably the General Secretary, Mr. F. H. Thompson, F.S.A., for undertaking its organization, and to thank all the contributors and those who attended for a very successful and informative occasion.

Index

Compiled by PHOEBE M. PROCTER